PRAISE FOR *GET A LIFE!*

'Rick Hughes' years of experience as a psychological counsellor have given him deep insights into what matters to people and what makes for a fulfilling life, both at work and home. This book provides us with access to these insights in an easily digestible and relatable way. He emphasises the importance of good relationships and communication and provides multiple case studies from his own experience. I highly recommend this book to help you reflect and put into practice some simple things that will improve your work–life harmony.'
David Roomes, Chief Medical Officer, Rolls-Royce

'This is a fantastic book to help guide thinking and contains practical tools to manage workplace pressures. It includes tips and ideas to enable us to develop skills to perform at our best both at home and at work and better navigate the ever-complex world of work. A superb book for individuals and organizations alike.'
Judith Grant, Director of Health and Wellbeing, Mace Group

'I'm delighted to fully endorse this well written book on a very important topic – our work–life balance. Rick Hughes has expertly accessed this topic with humour, insight and useful calls to action. His case studies provide the reader with a rich seam of experience which magnify and illustrate the key messages of the book. If the reader is looking for a book which is highly practical, superbly written and reaches the parts that others can't reach, then search no further!'
Andrew Kinder, Professional Head of Mental Health Services, Optima Health

'It is great to see a publication that explores such an interesting and engaging topic as work–life balance – one might even call it brave as this area is so personal and diverse, with a variety of meanings depending on where we are in our life. The content is well structured, engaging and practical and readers will all benefit from this book.'
Shaun Davis, Global Director of Safety, Health, Wellbeing and Sustainability, Royal Mail Group

Get a Life!

Creating a successful work–life balance

Rick Hughes

KoganPage

First published in Great Britain and the United States in 2020 by Kogan Page Limited

2nd Floor, 45 Gee Street
London
EC1V 3RS
United Kingdom

122 W 27th St, 10th Floor
New York, NY 10001
USA

4737/23 Ansari Road
Daryaganj
New Delhi 110002
India

www.koganpage.com

© Rick Hughes, 2020

The right of Rick Hughes to be identified as the author of this work has been asserted by him in accordance with the Copyright, Designs and Patents Act 1988.

ISBNs

Hardback   978 1 78966 202 3
Paperback   978 1 78966 200 9
Ebook   978 1 78966 201 6

British Library Cataloguing-in-Publication Data

A CIP record for this book is available from the British Library.

Library of Congress Cataloging-in-Publication Data

Names: Hughes, Rick, 1967- author.
Title: Get a life! : creating a successful work-life balance / Rick Hughes.
Description: London, United Kingdom ; New York, NY : Kogan Page, 2020. | Includes bibliographical references and index.
Identifiers: LCCN 2019052400 (print) | LCCN 2019052401 (ebook) | ISBN 9781789662023 (hardback) | ISBN 9781789662009 (paperback) | ISBN 9781789662016 (ebook)
Subjects: LCSH: Work-life balance. | Work and family.
Classification: LCC HD4904.25 .H84 2020 (print) | LCC HD4904.25 (ebook) | DDC 650.1–dc23
LC record available at https://lccn.loc.gov/2019052400
LC ebook record available at https://lccn.loc.gov/2019052401

Typeset by Integra Software Services, Pondicherry
Print production managed by Jellyfish
Printed and bound by CPI Group (UK) Ltd, Croydon, CR0 4YY

CONTENTS

Downloadable resources are available here:
www.koganpage.com/getalife

LIST OF FIGURES AND TABLES

Figures

Tables

FOREWORD

It's about getting a life

Rick Hughes' book *Get a Life!: Creating a successful work–life balance* explores a range of issues about how we might gain a balance in our working and personal lives. It encourages us to get some perspective in what we do and how we do it, to ensure that at the end of the day we get better job satisfaction without sacrificing our family, friends and important relationships in our lives. As Woody Allen once humorously put it: 'I don't want to achieve immortality through my work, I want to achieve it by not dying'!

The book is broken down into six main sections: your Personal Development, the People in your life, the Professional You, your Productivity and Performance, your Psychological and Physical Wellbeing, and then Practical Factors.

In Personal Development it is about having fun, reflecting on your experiences and having a spiritual side to your life (but not necessarily through religion). The People section highlights how important our relationships are in life, with our family, friends, work colleagues, etc, highlighting how you need to spend time managing these relationships to help yourself and your significant others. The Professional part of the book explores the purpose and meaning of work, coping with change at work and being more political to achieve your personal objectives.

Productivity and Performance is about how you should manage your hours of work, prioritizing your workload and managing your ambition. As John Ruskin once wrote in 1851: 'In order that people are happy in their work, these three things are needed: they must be fit for it, they must not do too much of it, and they must have a sense of success in it.' He highlights the overwhelming importance of psychological wellbeing; of having a sense of control and autonomy, asserting your needs, appreciating what you have, etc. And finally, in Practical Factors, Rick details some key aspects of our physical environments, management of finances, and engagement with information technologies that impact us in our work and non-work lives. The book closes with a concluding section entitled 'Pulling it all together', which will help you to scour the entirety of your work–life balance landscape.

Since the author is a seasoned psychological counsellor, he emphasizes the importance of going beyond just vision statements about health, wellbeing and work–life balance but says we all need to take personal and practical steps to achieve this vision as well. As the old Japanese proverb goes: 'Vision without action is a daydream, action without vision is a nightmare.'

This book is, yes, about action plans for 'getting a life' but it is primarily about getting some 'perspective' on your work and life. As Leonardo da Vinci wrote:

> Every now and then go away and have a little relaxation. To remain constantly at work will diminish your judgement. Go some distance away [psychologically he meant], because work will be in perspective and a lack of harmony is more readily seen.

We could all learn from this wise advice, as we can from reading this book.

Professor Sir Cary Cooper, CBE, ALLIANCE
Manchester Business School, University of Manchester

ACKNOWLEDGEMENTS

Grateful thanks to Debbie Dyker, Nick Edwards and Professor Ben Martin at the University of Aberdeen.

A huge thank you to the talented team at Kogan Page, with special mentions for Rebecca Bush and Anne-Marie Heeney who beautifully shaped this book with their insightful guidance and skilful editing.

A massive thanks to Kirsty, partly because she's my wonderful wife but also for being the perceptive first responder to all my drafts.

My indebted thanks to the many coaching, counselling and consultancy clients I've had the privilege of working with over 25 years.

And a final important thank you for the flexibility offered by my work commitments, enabling me to adopt a successful work–life balance to research and write this book.

Case studies

All case studies in this book, unless otherwise stated, are permissioned, disguised, adapted or composites, to protect confidentiality and anonymity.

Introduction

So you want to 'Get a Life'?

You've probably bought this book because you believe you could or need to improve your work–life balance. The good news is that this is all within your grasp. It might involve tweaking or adjusting aspects of your life or it could require some tough decisions and dramatic changes.

I'm going to take you on a journey through a series of pathways which will offer you choices and options. But only you can take the steps which suit you. With some coaching, insight and guidance, the future really is brighter.

There's no simple 'one-size-fits-all' because we are all unique individuals with a matrix of needs and wants, idiosyncratic personalities and behaviours, shaped within a complex family and social web, at different stages of careers in jobs that are peculiar to us and peppered with our own values, beliefs and norms.

So where do we start?

In the mid-1980s a daytime TV quiz show hit the UK screens. Hosted by Bob Holness, *Blockbusters* quickly became a favourite amongst students bunking off lectures to seek some televisual escapism from the arduous demands of opening the pages of a textbook (things have changed since then). In the show, a contestant would select a letter of the alphabet from a hexagonal block and Bob would ask a trivia question whose answer began with that letter. From this innocuous strategy emerged a classic phrase immortalized in television folklore, titillating viewers throughout the land when a contestant asked 'Can I have a P please, Bob?' Poor old Bob struggled to summon up a genuine smile each time.

Clearly still affected yet strangely inspired by this TV show, the sections of this book all begin with the letter P and for a good reason. It's to help nail to the flagpole the word PERSPECTIVE. Getting a life and creating a successful work–life balance is all about perspective. It's an attitude, approach, point of view and mindset. And it's one which is unique to each of us.

I remember meeting George, a former multinational executive who had amassed a sufficient pension to allow him to retire early. At the tender age of 55 he had an aspiration to continue working but in a role which gave him a new perspective; slowing down the pace, enjoying his Scottish rural life, meeting people he wouldn't normally meet and contributing to the lives of others. So he managed to get a job as a delivery driver for one of the major supermarkets and tootled off in his fancy liveried van to stock the households of fine Aberdeenshire folk.

Unfortunately for George, he told me this was one of the most stressful jobs ever! He had an impossible driving schedule, struggled with an unreliable satnav, frequently got lost or stuck down muddy farm tracks and found that when he did reach customers they'd either not be in or would complain about the groceries selected by the store. He lasted a month.

And yet Tony, who delivers groceries to us, albeit from a different supermarket, and is clearly motivated by lovely customers like us, absolutely loves his job!

It's all about perspective.

The first chapter of this book involves Personal Development, and delves into the individual characteristics, behaviours, attitudes and skills which shape how we engage with the world around us in our own inimitable way.

Then we move into People. Humans are social creatures and our whole lives are influenced by our relationships with partners, parents, perhaps children, wider family and friends, plus those with whom we work. It is said that we can choose our friends but we can't choose our family. Actually, we can rarely choose our work colleagues either.

The third chapter that's crucial to mediating our work–life balance covers Professional Issues: how we engage with, treat and evolve in our working lives. A job is far more than just a job. For some people it defines them, for others it gives them a reason to get up in the morning and, of course, work can provide the financial means to influence our affluence.

It can be *how* we do our jobs which can significantly influence the economy by which we sail through or struggle with life at work. Productivity and Performance is an important chapter which focuses on key skills involving efficiency, planning and prioritizing. If we can work more with less effort, then we're going to have the capability to choose what to do with the rest of our time.

But it's not all about work. Our Psychological and Physical Wellbeing barometers our ability to function, physically and mentally, contributes to a sense of resilience and helps us to manage the ups and down of what life throws at us. How we slide along the pressure/stress continuum allows us to handle situations with relative ease... or not.

The sixth chapter on Practical Factors deals with the key functional aspects of our home, work and physical environment. A work–life balance cannot ignore our attitude and behaviour towards money and finances so budgeting and financial planning is summed up here. We can't escape the social media, information technology and communications revolution either. But our approach towards this can determine whether it works for us... or against us.

At the end of each chapter, there is a work–life balance scaling system which gives you the opportunity to consider areas that require attention. In the final chapter, Pulling It All Together, you can plot the total scores from each previous chapter to enable you to plan and prioritize actions for improving (and maintaining) your work–life balance.

Whilst this book seeks to provide a work–life balance perspective for you to make the choices and changes that can improve your life, it may take PATIENCE and PRACTICE. But if you take one step at a time, you'll start to build a momentum which can launch you on a trajectory of transformation.

The best way to start is to begin.

01
Personal development

Rest and relaxation

It is a lovely way to start: focusing on how we rest and relax. And yet few of us can easily identify what makes us chilled out, let alone actually do it. We live on an adrenaline overdrive: bombarded by a frenetic pace of life and a visual, auditory and information overload from work and family demands, current affairs and entertainment, smartphones and social media.

Most of us say we are relaxed when we're at home with our feet up watching TV. But unless it's watching a documentary of cute meerkats, a lot of TV is also stressful. We like to be scared by horror films; cry over weepy romantic dramas; become informed (or depressed) by current affairs; excite ourselves with action movies; or find entertainment in a competitive dance-off... and yet there's stress in much of this. Even meerkats struggle in life.

Of course, many of us find we don't concentrate fully on our TV feast because we're tapping into tablets, self-diagnosing our TV-triggered migraine, or messaging friends and family on social media (even if they're in the next room). And, as we'll discuss in the section about social media (Chapter 6), much of the time we're secretly envying other people who are pretending that they're having a much better life than us.

At school we're taught the maths of trigonometry, the history of Ancient Greece, the biology of osmosis or the physics of gravity – but when do we learn how to rest and relax? How do we stop, breathe out, take a break and recharge our batteries?

We need to de-clutter, cleanse and purify our head-space so we can empty the junk that we keep in its place. If we're not being stimulated by life, then we're lost in a debt of worry about things from the past we regret doing, or not doing. Or, we're twitching with anxiety about things that haven't happened yet and which may never happen, at least not in the dramatically negative way we catastrophize.

Susan

Susan was a client of mine who came for counselling 'stressed'. When we started to peel back the onion layers, she realized that she 'needed to be busy to be worthy', and this set in motion a tsunami of unrealistic activities, demands and quests which had the completely opposite effect. She failed to achieve anything except anxiety-triggered eczema. When we worked on putting her back on the map and focused on self-worth, she found her salvation came in appreciating that it wasn't about 'doing' but 'being'. For her this meant being at peace with herself, and her antidote was to seek out what contributed to her rest and relaxation. She identified walking in the local botanical gardens and learning about plants, taking a class on creative writing and swimming at lunchtimes.

Rest and relaxation is not necessarily about inactivity. Rather it is about what offers a personal nourishment to the junk food of frenetic life.

A client I saw recently told me that when she felt stressed, she would knit using different coloured wools. I asked her what she was knitting and she explained that she didn't know… she just continued without any plan, script or pattern. The outcome wasn't important but it had become her perpetual journey of relaxation.

Rest involves finding a balance to the behaviours or activities that allow us to rewind, recharge and regroup, physically and mentally. Crucially, it's about building this into a daily schedule so we look forward to the slots in our day which offer this relaxation sustenance. Even the mere conscious recognition that we are actively choosing to do something that is badged 'rest and relaxation' (R&R) has the effect of making us absorb the benefits.

Work–life balance action
Rest and relaxation

Identify what could contribute to your R&R. Make sure it is achievable, and realistic within your working week. This could include:

- walking round the block at lunchtime;
- trips to the gym or swimming pool before or after work;
- having a time after dinner when you read a book, listen to music or focus on your own private time.

People even tell me that ironing or cleaning can be cathartic, so even though it might be a functional activity, if your mind is focused on this as 'down-time' you'll treat it as such.

Next, schedule a plan for a week in the near future, leaving some wriggle room to adapt to situations which may crop up, those which might require you to change your plans.

The secret here is that you're only planning an R&R strategy for *one week*. This removes any pressure to perform, or any anxiety about needing to structure this into your life forever.

At the end of the week, schedule time to reflect on how you felt during that week. In most cases, you'll be able to acknowledge the value and benefits of your R&R time, which will hopefully motivate you to put it back on the agenda for the next week. One week at a time can quickly turn into months, and before you know it, it will be your way of being.

What further adds to our capacity to relax is leading a healthy lifestyle. It's proving to us that we're important... our mind and bodies are important. This means attending to what's now referred to as 'sleep hygiene' but in the old days was simply about getting a good night's sleep. Good sleep is often compromised by the blue lights of tablets and smartphones; as you may know, this interferes with the body's natural sleep-inducing chemicals.

As well as having good sleep hygiene, it also means getting enough exercise to maintain the right weight and fitness level and avoid putting undue pressure on our bodies. Then, we want to be maintaining a healthy, balanced diet. Many people find this threatening, because it sounds boring or means they can't eat some treats now and again – but don't panic, the key is about diet being *balanced*.

Mindfulness and living in the moment

A major threat to R&R is that we're always thinking ahead: the parent/teachers meeting on Monday night; the presentation on Tuesday; getting the car into the garage on Wednesday; Aunt Mabel's birthday event on Thursday; the review with our boss on Friday; let alone what we're going to have for tea tonight. Our activity radar branches into our short-term future and saturates our minds. It could trigger anxiety and foreboding or a sense of dread, all of which is unnecessary to what's actually going on in the present moment.

Then, if we're not preoccupied with the future, we're anchored down by the past – ruminating over things we said or did, or should have said or done. Or we may still be trapped by difficult, upsetting or traumatic events from the past which we haven't yet found a way to process. It's not about forcing these into a hidden internal vault – though arguably, this can work for some – but it's about suspending the intrusiveness of these events so they don't unnecessarily punctuate our daily lives. There's a time and a place for everything. And dwelling on the past doesn't change what has happened.

A key part of a work–life balance is finding the time to be present. This can require discipline and practice but is very much worth the effort – because it *does* work. It involves suspending thoughts or internal chatter and the merry-go-round of spiralling thinking.

One of my counsellor colleagues, Sha'yo Lai, has integrated Eastern and Western philosophies to evolve a mindful approach to daily living. Mindfulness owes much of its origins to Buddhist teachings as a way to develop wisdom and self-knowledge. This involves bringing a conscious awareness or focused attention to our thoughts, feelings and bodily sensations in relation to the world around us in the moment. It's a grounding way to connect and root ourselves in the moment in a way that embellishes and enriches the minutest of experiences.

Work–life balance action
Mindfulness

The simple model involves attending to your senses: what you see, hear, touch, smell and taste. You can do this in a quiet room or anywhere you find yourself on your own, even in your car or walking to a meeting.

First, get yourself into a relaxed state by monitoring and controlling your breathing. Take a breath in through your nose over the count of five, then hold for four, then out through your mouth for six. Do this a few times and you'll notice your slow, steady breathing starts to relax you and lowers your heart rate.

Next, consciously spend a few moments orientating yourself to your surroundings:

- What do you see around you? The colours, shapes, contrasts or visual connections.

- Focus on what you hear – not just what's immediately audible, but the background smorgasbord of noises, the sirens, the birds, the laughter or chatter, the central heating or air conditioning, a clock ticking, a plane overhead or a creaky floorboard.

- Attend to what you feel and sense – the temperature, the feel of your skin or hands, sensation and sensitivity.

- What can you smell? Can you identify what the smells are and do they represent a mix? As you move around, can you smell the changes in your environment?

- And finally, taste. What did you last eat that you can still taste in your mouth, or how does your coffee actually taste? When

> you have your next meal, savour the flavour rather than just shovelling it down as fast as you can.
>
> All of this will help to orient you in the present. If you're out for a walk, seek out what you wouldn't normally. Look up and around, open your mind, open your senses.

Roger

Roger, a director at a pharmaceutical company, has the luxury of his own office. Each lunch time, he flips the venetian blinds, sticks his phone on silent, and spends 15 minutes mindfully connecting with his senses. Even though it's the same office each time, he explained to me that there's always something new about the experience. This short quarter-hour exercise allows him to unwind, take stock, be in the moment and refresh his mind for the afternoon ahead.

Acceptance and commitment

Aligned to the practice of mindfulness is the idea of not fighting intrusive thoughts, mental clutter and distractions. They are what they are. We often think we have no control over our thoughts – but they're just thoughts, and we *can* overrule and replace them with alternative ones.

Much of the conflict that exists within us is the fight between a critical or judgemental thought and a rational part of us which is trying to challenge this negativity. Once we can accept that both can co-exist, we reduce the tension of the conflict which exists from this cognitive sparring.

When we have a physical pain, we either take some medicine or head over to our doctor and seek their wise counsel to remedy the situation. We resist pain because we think it is bad. But pain serves an important function: to warn us about an injury or to take the foot off the gas and recuperate. Society has developed this fixation that the medical profession will cure us of all our ailments, but the first thing that medics learn in training is 'do no harm'... in other words, sometimes the first or best thing that Western medicine will do is *nothing*. This isn't always exactly how we see it! Medicine can't solve everything and despite their skills and commitment, medics can't always fix us. As soon as we take some responsibility for our own health and wellbeing, we release ourselves from the, perhaps impossible, need to feel no pain. And the same can apply with mental health or psychological pain.

Of course, pain relief in different forms might be imperative in situations that require it, including with chronic, debilitating physical pain or post-trauma psychological pain. However, there's strong research evidence that in both chronic pain and psychological trauma, an acceptance strategy can help to resist the battle to mitigate the effects. We learn to live with it by accepting it.

Acceptance strategies are important in developing a work–life balance. Sometimes we're going to be spinning too many plates at one time, where the demands on us exceed our ability to cope. The balance comes from recognizing this conflict, and accepting that it's temporary, or that one step at a time to make incremental changes might be all that's required.

Gregor

Gregor was a successful sales executive for a business supplies firm. He was great at building relationships with his customers and was sublime in the one-to-one discussions, identifying needs in a personable manner and finding a client-centred way to pull it all together. Yet when he had to give presentations to more than a handful or people, his anxiety would trigger him to blush, his voice quaver and his hands shake. He hated himself for this and expressed massive frustration about being totally fine in one situation and a quivering wreck in others.

When we worked on this and sought to accept the differences which were creating the internal conflict, he found he was able to accept and rationalize reasons for the discrepancy. He adapted his public speaking into a style which spoke 'with' his audience rather than 'to' them, but which also accepted the normal, positive anxiety which enabled him to keep focused in what were important pitches.

We're not always going to be able to resolve something which might be inhibiting us. We fight the unfightable, determined to find a solution. And yet maybe the battle can be won by accepting the inhibitions. This is a crucial aspect of appreciating who we are, and loving who we are. There's always going to be someone smarter than us, more good-looking, better at presenting or managing, possessing social skills we'd dream of and able to deal with stressful situations we marvel at. Good for them. But we're not them. To be accepting of ourselves, with the good and the bad, allows us to resist the stubborn quest to be perfect, which is impossible anyway.

Don

Don was in his 50s when he came to see me. Agitated and flustered, within moments of sitting down he launched into his story about hitting a mid-life crisis. He was resisting the signs of aging with all manner of lotions and potions, spending a small fortune in the process. When he stopped, I paused to summarize his predicament. But before I could condense what I had heard, I saw his gaze shift from my eyes to the top of my head to my receding tuft which was all that was left from what was, in my younger years, a fine head of hair. I knew where he was going and I smiled. And in my smile he recognized that at a similar age to him, I was not fighting hair loss or masking it with some ridiculous comb-over. I accepted it. He laughed and so began his journey of acceptance. I didn't need to say much during that session; my hair, or lack of it, spoke for me.

Personal creativity

As we saw in the last section, we can benefit from accepting how things are and not battling with a 'problem' that we'll never fix. But it's not all about accepting and doing nothing. There's much that we *can* do to transform our lives, and particularly in relation to a work–life balance.

Take creativity, for instance. We all have buckets of creativity within us, even if much of this is directed to our work. What we lose from this is the wider dexterity of creativity which can blossom further in our non-work lives. Like most of what we cover in this book, creating a successful work–life balance isn't always about splitting the work and non-work domains of our lives, but about bringing the two together, and allowing one to feed and nourish the other.

Paul

Paul came to see me, feeling apathetic about work and lacking motivation and inspiration. When I asked about his non-work life, he explained he was an expert 'gamer'; in fact, he was in the global top 50 best players for that particular interactive computer game. I invited him to identify the characteristics of what he felt as a gamer and he included words such as 'connection', 'respect', 'professionalism', 'aptitude' and 'excitement'. I asked what would need to happen for those words to be associated with work, and he was able to come up with a set of realistic ways in which this could happen. Once he started seeing it this way, that single session was sufficient for him to understand how his non-work creativity could suddenly kick-start his work life.

Anne

On the other side of the coin, I remember Anne had just survived a threat of redundancy at her work. The possibility of losing her job made her confront her belief that she had, and was, nothing apart from her job. This made her appreciate the need to build up her non-work persona, and within a few sessions she stumbled into an unrecognized creative passion for creating colouring-in books for adults.

Whether it is in your work, or non-work, how can you crank up your creative juices and unleash an unrecognized part of you? You'll know when you've found something because you won't want to stop doing it. You don't have to be an expert, but you do need to enjoy it. The mere appreciation of the enjoyment will add a further layer to your work–life balance tapestry.

I've seen creativity blossoming in so many walks of life. My neighbour's garden that puts mine to shame. The friend who runs our local charity shop who is able to display so many goods so well in such a confined space. The various locals who pitch their wares at our area's producers' market, including one who seems to pay her mortgage by making intricate embroidered pouches of lavender.

At work, I see creativity in how people resolve problems. Or I marvel at the way that online TED speakers can nail an issue so succinctly. And even the creativity that politicians employ to expertly answer a question without actually giving an answer.

As you start to consider where your new-found creativity might lie, it can take several attempts and some wrong turns. At the age of 10, I thought I had the creative ability to pick up a clarinet and make beautiful music. The response by the fleeing family cat suggested otherwise.

But it is about giving things a go. Even something that doesn't work for you might open up a variation which could work (although I've since found that I have no creative potential with any musical instruments!). Whatever we do, we need to enjoy it.

One of the best places to start is to think back to the things you enjoyed as a kid. Or scout around and identify what other people are doing. From the producers' market I visited recently, I had a fascinating conversation with someone selling his heather honey. He spoke about his work nurturing his bees, looking after the beehives and driving them up remote Highland glens to find the heather hotspots. It felt like a real collaborative effort with nature. This conversation really resonated with me, emerging from my childhood fascination with insects and creepy-crawlies, together with memories of my grandfather's apiculture hobby, nurturing his cluster of beehives.

Creativity is not limited to things we 'make'; rather, it's how we engage our brains to plumb a creative depth. Many people enjoy being part of book clubs, where the group chooses to read a book then discuss what it meant to them when they meet. Here, it's about a creative interpretation, where everyone will bring something different to the table.

Much of creativity is about self-interpretation, expression and creating a meaning behind a perspective. A colleague of mine attends a monthly 'collage' group where she pores over magazines to select images to make a collage or mosaic to craft some personal message or piece of art. Another is a fiddle player in a Scottish ceilidh band where each member brings a different variation to traditional dance pieces.

Creativity also involves problem solving, which can be a part of life at work or beyond. Again, how we learn to be creative transcends boundaries, so a capacity to be creative in one domain often jumps ship to the other.

John works as a mechanical engineer fixing trucks and yet he found his problem-solving skills enabled him to be creative with a team that rescued landed dolphins, developing hydraulic inflatable flotation devices. Similarly, Fraser worked with community youth groups finding creative ways to maintain attendance, focus and enthusiasm, and this experience helped him secure work managing teams of volunteers for a charity.

From a work–life balance perspective, creativity can also be experienced by the judicial use of 'down-time' such as commuting to and from work. Rather than seeing this as wasted time, losing ourselves in social media or listening out for news headlines and traffic reports, there's an opportunity to be creative. On my drive in and out of work, I'm trying to learn Portuguese and recently was weirdly gratified to find myself emitting a Portuguese expletive when a driver nearly swerved into me.

Others find down-time as an opportunity to be mindful, accepting everything as part of the here and now.

Adventure and excitement

Creativity doesn't need to stop at hobbies or pastimes. Creativity can evolve into adventure and excitement. If we do what we've always done, we'll get what we always got. Meaning, if we don't push our boundaries, try new things and take risks, then we won't experience the highs of what life can offer. Of course, this can also expose us to risk, threat and feelings of vulnerability – but if we can accept these as part of what's necessary to reap the benefits of new experiences, then it's usually well worth it.

Some of us can be risk-averse and take the safe options. There's nothing wrong with this in itself. But now and again we all need a gentle nudge into the unknown to enliven our lot and allow us to experience something new. Some risk aversion can come from things we have done before and suffered a loss as a result. Or it might come from a judgemental attitude of someone important to us. Both can be mitigated by managing risk or zapping thoughts of judgement.

Adventure and excitement is not limited to paddling down the Amazon in a dug-out canoe, though I have no doubt this would be both adventurous and exciting, my abysmal swimming skills aside. But it is about pushing our boundaries and taking us out of our comfort zone.

In recent years, there's been a fascination with creating a 'bucket list'; the ambitions and quests we might want to experience before we die. People I know who have drafted such a list found they were continually revamping and adding to it. One great experience seems to propel ambition to something else and something new. It becomes a constant revival of adventure, excitement and drive.

Max

A number of years ago, Max came to see me because of his frustration with what he described as introversion. He was a computer programmer so his work world didn't involve much social interaction or adventure. His 'stuckness' emerged from frustration – not so much from being introverted, but because he felt trapped and wanted to be 'set free'. We evolved a spider diagram, much like a bucket list, of all the things that he would find exciting and captivating, irrespective of ability or cost. The idea was to open up his capacity to experience. OK, so his quest to walk on the moon was never likely to materialize… but many of the other ambitions offered a ray of hope.

This work with Max enabled me to see the value in 'thinking big', because it opens up what may be a shut door of opportunity. The reality check can come later but for now, think the impossible dream. I met Max a few years later and he reminded me of some of his dreams. One was to go deep-sea fishing. This never happened – but he did end up fishing by rowing boat in Scottish lochs, and actually stumbled across a new freshwater species of fish. He showed me the proud photo of him and his fishy friend with the new species named on a card next to it.

When he originally saw me, he also reflected on feeling stagnated about never having left his small suburban town. He dreamt of travelling the world. Since then, he had taken an amazing volunteer opportunity in Thailand looking after a breed of monkey whose name I will never remember. More recently, he had been living in Denmark with his partner, making websites for his community. Max, formerly paralysed by introversion, had taken risks and used his dreamscape to launch into new opportunities and amazing experiences.

What Max ended up doing may *seem* like an exception to the rule – but I dispute that. As I said in the introduction, it's all about perspective. Great things can come from unexpected places.

In my first, albeit short career, I worked in a provincial advertising agency in Scotland, working on accounts which failed to give me any real excitement or satisfaction. I started to grow frustrated with what I felt was the commercialization of persuading people to buy something they didn't really need.

And then just before I quit, the agency won a contract from a hero of mine, Jackie Stewart, the three-times Formula 1 Grand Prix motor-racing champion. As a young lad into cars, this sounded like a dream come true. Resisting the urge to quit my job, I threw everything into this role. The brief was to promote the Jackie Stewart Shooting School at the world-famous Gleneagles Hotel and involved several meetings with him to work on the project. I remember one of these meetings was with him in his hotel suite one Sunday morning when the Monaco Grand Prix was on TV in the background. Now and again he'd jump up and berate a particularly stupid driving error. I'd have paid good money just to experience that.

Anyway, we created really effective promotional material. Jackie very kindly thanked me for this by flying me (well, his pilot did) in his private jet down to Milton Keynes, where his Grand Prix team was based, for a sponsor's 'dinner'. An absolutely amazing experience emerged from my depths of despair.

Having said that, the contract came to an end, the account closed and I left the agency for a new career as a therapist. All good for all concerned. (I'd like to say I have Jackie's personal number on speed-dial… but I don't. If you're reading this, thank you very much Jackie!)

I do recognize that Jackie is not going to be offering everyone this sort of experience, and I was in the right place at the right time and incredibly lucky. But we can all push the boat out, as Max did literally on his fishing adventure, and do something different and new that provides us with an enriching experience. And the great thing is that it is often the things we stumble into by chance that offer us the most unexpected opportunities.

This is where it factors into our work–life balance. Nourishing experiences can emerge from both work and non-work opportunities;

it's about being open to them, and taking a chance. One of the phrases of wisdom that my grandmother shared with me was, 'It's better to have loved and lost than never to have loved at all'. This resonates, not just with love and relationships, but also about taking risks and stepping out of that comfort zone. Notwithstanding health and safety considerations, what's the worst that could happen? What might you gain? And how amazing might you feel afterwards?

Stages in life, changes and life events

In plotting your bucket list or spider diagram dreamscape, undoubtedly you'll be considering your capabilities based on your age and abilities. As we age, many of us will lose physical attributes, but gain perspective and wisdom. We might become slightly more risk-averse, but gain an increase in affluence to give us more choice. We might lose a carefree attitude of youth, but gain confidence and direction.

We can't escape the passage of time and the impact of life experiences. As we get older, we accumulate more varied experiences, good and bad. Each will impact our assessment of risk and responsibility; but they shouldn't thwart ambition, opportunity or potential. Life has a habit of throwing us unexpected traumas. It's unrealistic to think otherwise. But it's how we deal with, process, learn and move on from them that helps us develop a resilience for the future.

A work–life balance is constantly changing, and we need to be calibrating that balance in view of the changes that are occurring around us.

Reflecting on how we have dealt with past changes (or not) allows us to inoculate ourselves against future shifts. Using the Life Stage Audit below can help us consider how we have dealt with changing stages in life, and how we might prepare for future stages.

Work–life balance action
Life stage audit

Think back to stages of your life so far and identify any major events, traumas, conflicts or other crises you may have experienced. (If you choose to write this down, you don't need to show this to anyone, or justify what you write down – any experience that had an impact on you counts.) Consider:

- How did you resolve or get through the experience? Was there a resolution?
- What did you learn from the experience? What insight have you gained?

When you have considered each life stage up to your current one, look forward into the life stages to come:

- What conflicts, threats or crises might come up for each life stage? (Try to be realistic, and strike a balance between overly optimistic – nothing will ever faze you ever again! – and overly pessimistic – you're doomed and life holds nothing but stress from here on out!)
- What opportunities do you see happening for each future stage?

With any change in life stage we experience losses and gains. It's important to recognize, appreciate and accept both. We may remember our first day at primary school mixed with anticipation and dread: losing some security of home, yet marking a new time of socialization. At college, university or our first job, whilst losing the structured order of school we may have gained greater self-responsibility. In relationships, we gain love and companionship, but must also learn to work with our partner rather than independently in some situations.

At work, every promotion or job change means we lose some of the familiarity of tasks and colleagues, but they also offer new potential and opportunity.

It's important to reflect on the losses and gains, because these help us to balance the reality of life experiences and their impact on us. To ignore a loss means we might deny a need to process and mark that transition, just like mourning the loss of a loved one. Equally, to ignore a gain means we miss out on the joy of that gain, the satisfaction of an achievement, or the celebration of happiness.

Andrew and Sally

Andrew and Sally came to see me for couples' counselling. Four years into their marriage, they felt they were reaching a point of incompatibility, pushing each others' buttons negatively and generally seeking opportunities to annoy or blame the other. It reached the point that, on holiday in Greece, they couldn't agree to do something together, so they stormed off to do their own things – Sally wanting a day out to see the Acropolis and Andrew preferring to read his book at the hotel pool.

In counselling, we realized that in the quest to be a unified unit, both had ignored their individual interests and needs, and so felt frustrated. Andrew and Sally learnt to accept their differences in personality and motivations, realizing the importance of finding space and independence within their shared experiences as a couple. They were able to learn about and enjoy their differences rather than feel conflicted by them.

Life events will have a huge impact on our work–life balance. A bereavement of someone close to us might generate a shift in our values and beliefs. We might find that through mourning, we focus on our own mortality and the choices we are making at that time.

Nicky

When Nicky came to see me after her mother died of cancer, she had overcome the initial shock of the loss but was now in a more reflective stage of questioning everything in her life. 'What's important has changed' she explained. Her retail job was her life, and she had loved the supervisory role she'd worked hard to achieve. And yet the bereavement triggered her to reflect on family, how she had suspended her wish to have a child of her own and neglected her nieces and nephews. She changed her work–life balance; she stayed in her job but made time for herself and her family as well and she encouraged her team to do the same. Her own change in work–life balance priorities had benefits for her colleagues too.

Emotional intelligence

One barrier to finding a work–life balance can be poor, ineffective or misunderstood communication skills. We miss what we are saying or skew what we hear so that the communication exchange fails. Accuracy of communication creates an economy of time; we get from A to B more quickly.

Active listening (and communication skills)

It's a tough skill to listen, really *actively* listen. The traditional Chinese character for the verb 'to listen' absorbs qualities within it involving to hear, think, see, focus and feel. This helps us to understand listening as more than just hearing and involves much more than we might consider. Next time you're listening to someone talking to you, reflect on the extent to which you're engaging these competencies.

There's much we can do to demonstrate that we are listening, but it's not about faking it: people know when we're not being real and transparent. This is part of the art of listening – we have to engage actively.

It can be an odd experience talking to someone who simply stares at you, motionless, without any acknowledgement of what you're saying. Try it with someone; it's really off-putting! Most of us learn to adopt the process of 'minimal encouraging' where we make supportive noises to let the other person know we're following them, but without interrupting their flow. This is chipping in with things like 'uh-huh', 'mmm', 'yeah', 'ah' etc. We usually supplement these with non-verbal affirmations, such as with a smile, nod, tilt of the head, mirroring of the speaker's posture, a slight frown to reflect concentration, and so on.

An effective way to demonstrate you have understood what has been said, or to seek clarification, is to reflect back or mirror what you've heard. This may involve paraphrasing the words and also including any meaning or emotion behind them. If someone says 'I'm so stressed after that meeting', you might pick up a more subconscious essence or deeper nuances of what they're saying by replying 'I can see that meeting really frustrated you, it didn't go as you planned'. You have resonated a deeper understanding of that person's 'stress'.

Open-ended questions allow the recipient to expand on their response as opposed to closed questions which tend to elicit a 'yes' or 'no' answer. A closed question can also steer a desired response. 'Are you stressed?' can be a well-meaning question from a simple observation of someone's behaviour, but it can also come across as an insinuation, judgement or opinion. Whereas the more open-ended 'how are you feeling?' allows the recipient a choice over how to respond and with what. Questions with 'why?' can sometimes be interpreted as judgemental: 'why are you stressed?' Words like 'how' and 'what' can be softer interrogatives: 'how are things?' or 'what's going on for you these days?'

When you are managing a situation either at work or at home, summarizing a perspective clarifies your understanding and pulls together the key issues. This can be particularly helpful when a conversation is becoming more heated. Though we all need to express our frustrations now and again, we need to choose the right time and place for this. By summarizing the key points someone has made, you can demonstrate that you have listened to them and they can reclarify if you have misunderstood something.

It might be appropriate in some circumstances to challenge the other person with any inconsistencies in what they are saying, thinking, feeling or doing. A person might tell you they are cool, calm and collected, but their body language can tell you otherwise (tense facial muscles, clenched fists, perspiring forehead etc). This may need to be handled delicately and sensitively, using your ears, heart, mind, eyes and attentiveness to listen, as contained in the Chinese symbol.

Work–life balance action
Active listening

A fun way to practise 'active listening' is the dyad exercise. With another person, one of you talks to the other for five minutes. The listener should not use any words, simply demonstrating their listening non-verbally. Then swap over. It's difficult!

Verbal messages

What we say and, importantly, how we say it, can have a significant impact on a work–life balance because it allows us to navigate the choppy communication waters more effectively. I would argue that at least a third of what we say or hear incorrectly contributes to stress at work – which we'll probably take home, where it can preoccupy our thoughts and feed our anxieties or frustrations. The better we can say what we mean, the more likely we are to get what we seek or need. The majority of conflict stems from poor and ineffective communication and whilst we don't want to be too robotic, thinking before we speak can save time on clarification.

There are probably 101 ways we can say things. The key is being able to say the right thing in the right way at the right time. This may take time and practice. It is worth appreciating and understanding what we say and how this could be interpreted in a way we might not intend. There are a number of ways we might express things. Some may be more appropriate in one context and not another, depending on what's going on. The key is intentionality. Do we mean or intend to say what we say? The following are some of the ways we might say things:

- directing and leading – taking control of a situation and directing the focus;
- judging – coming across as judgemental, opinionated or critical;
- accepting – an appreciation or understanding of the other or what they say;
- evaluating statements – comments loaded with accusatory or loaded opinion;
- empathizing – as if you are walking in the shoes of the other;
- blaming language – finger-pointing and accusing, often steeped in anger or frustration;
- moralizing – presenting your own values and morals on the perspective of the other;
- labelling and diagnosing – assuming we have the skills to diagnose when we don't;
- respectful listening – being attentive to the other, demonstrated with respect;
- non-accepting – failing to accept the perspectives of the other in favour of self;
- spacing – using noises to keep the conversation, eg 'um', 'er', 'what was I going to say?' etc;
- assurance-seeking – such as 'do you know what I mean?' or 'do you follow me?';

- advising or teaching – when educating from a position of greater wisdom or expertise;
- belittling – a condescending or deprecating remark, loaded with power imbalance;
- over-interpreting – going overboard with a quest to assign meaning or understanding;
- interrupting – jumping into conversations before others have finished;
- interrogating – overly harsh or necessary questioning beyond what is appropriate;
- parallel – usurping your lived experience over that of the other;
- faking – over-egging genuineness and transparency with over-the-top gestures.

You'll probably have a clutch of additional observations concerning verbal exchanges. Much of this emerges from life experience, meeting lots of different people but also the intuition or 'gut-response' that helps us sense beyond the consciousness. We can feel when something is not right or when what someone says doesn't match up with what you feel. This incongruence emerges from the emotional intelligence we develop throughout our lives.

Emotional regulation

How we manage, engage with or project our emotions has a massive impact on our work–life balance. Being more emotionally 'intelligent' helps us to mediate the ebbs and flows of life at home and work. Conversely, misfiring emotionally can have consequences for us and those with whom we connect.

A key foundation of emotional regulation is the ability to understand our own personal emotional repertoire or language, and in so doing, to understand others. In other words, to effectively and accurately empathize.

Utilizing our emotional toolbox requires us to develop a conscientious and systematic quest of self-understanding. How do we engage our emotions and when? How and why do we

respond the way we do? Do we react without thinking, sponta-
neously; or do we pause, reflect, gather the evidence and express
a considered emotional response? For many of us, it's often the
former – but emotional regulation is working towards the latter.

Anger

Anger is a primal emotion, crucial to warning us of impending
threats and danger – though it's probably the one emotion we
struggle with most. Many of us shy away from what we perceive as
'conflict' and in so doing resist the right we might have to express
or assert 'anger'. This can be influenced by culture and how we
perceive society normalizes or permits our expression of anger. It
can be further tarnished by issues from the past that illuminate 'red
flags' or press our trigger buttons – in other words, we might react,
not because of the here-and-now issue, but because we have unre-
solved anger-related issues. Furthermore, we can project our anger
inadvertently on the wrong people or even project issues we are
angry about ourselves onto others. It can get complicated.

Rhona and Ralph

I remember working with Rhona, a live-at-home mother of two boys aged
11 and 12. Her husband Ralph worked away a lot, but did what he could to
join forces and do 'family stuff' when home. Ralph had expressed concern
about how he felt Rhona was being overly angry towards the boys and
had suggested counselling. Somewhat resistant at first, Rhona felt there
was nothing wrong with her. This was actually my view too… there was
nothing wrong with her. In our work, she did admit to going 'a bit over the
top', sometimes snapping at the children. What emerged was a deeper
resentment towards Ralph and what she perceived as his freedom at
work whilst she was left to look after the home and their children. She
was projecting her jealousy towards Ralph and her frustration about
missing her former work life on the children. Once she could discern her
emotional cues, she could direct them more appropriately.

Vocabulary of emotions

Like the concept of 'stress' – where pressure to me might be stress for someone else – how we interpret emotions can differ between us all. It can be useful to consider semantics and get behind our meaning and perception of a particular emotion.

Our vocabulary of emotions gives us choices and options to better define what we are experiencing emotionally in a given moment. Have a look through the chart in Table 1.1 and see if any of the words better encapsulate or present a more accurate definition of an emotion in a moment in time. Clearly we're not going to be whipping out this chart and finger-pointing to a specific emotional cue when we 'get emotional'… but it's worth reflecting on the choices and options.

Work–life balance action
Emotional intensity

Consider the degree of emotional intensity in your repertoire or vocabulary of emotional expression. Identifying the most accurate intensity allows us to emotionally regulate and express a more appropriate meaning.

Table 1.1   Vocabulary of emotions

	ANGER	HAPPINESS	FEAR
High Intensity	Fuming	Ecstatic	Terrified
	Rage	Euphoric	Paralysed
	Seething	Exhilarated	Petrified
Medium Intensity	Annoyed	Cheerful	Afraid
	Irritated	Elated	Scared
	Spiteful	Buoyant	Nervous
Low Intensity	Irked	Genial	Anxious
	Disappointed	Satisfied	Tense
	Dismayed	Content	Uneasy

This reflects that we have three degrees of emotional intensity from strong, through medium to light. For example, when we are angry, we could describe our feelings as 'infuriated' (strong), 'irritated' (medium) or 'dismayed' (light). This intensity rating and definition can really help construct a more accurate meaning of our emotions – which might in turn give us options as to how to respond and react.

Spirituality, religion, belief and faith

From a work–life balance perspective, if we have a faith, religion or belief, we need to find the time to express or devote ourselves. This may emerge from formal places and times of worship or prayer or from a wider 'way of being' in how we live our lives. We can schedule specific chunks of time or, as with mindfulness, grab the few moments necessary to find that personal connection or space.

Can we live our lives without spirituality, religion, belief and faith? Possibly. Many readers will claim they do so and still lead a 'good life'. Indeed, the former Bishop of Edinburgh, Dr Richard Holloway, claims in his book *Godless Morality* that it could be the ultimate triumph and achievement of all religions for people to choose not to be spiritual, religious, a believer or a purveyor of faith and yet still contribute actively and positively to a morally supportive, stable and loving society.

Ali

Ali came to see me when she was in her final year at university, stressed about her final exams and anxious about what she should be doing when she finished her studies. Whilst we worked on some anxiety management and exam revision strategies, she alluded to her faith as being a strong guide for her way of being. She was able to divest some of her future-focused anxiety onto her belief that her God would help her find 'her way'. This immediately cleared her pathway for exam revision, and reinforced the stability she derived from her faith.

Jacquie and Sally

When Jacquie's husband died, she felt like she'd lost a limb, bereft of the person with whom she had shared 50 years of marriage. A 'non-believer', as she put it, she found comfort, community and companionship from her local church and found a new faith with it.

And yet when I worked with Sally after her divorce, she felt her religious beliefs had trapped her in a psychologically damaging relationship where the notion of divorce was regarded as a 'sin' and therefore unacceptable. She left her husband and entered what could be described as a more Humanist way of living, where she was able to respect different religions whilst divorcing herself also of her former 'restrictive' (her words) faith.

As a counsellor and coach, I work to empower my clients to find their own solutions, and create the changes they seek. Traditionally, this means taking some control over a situation which might appear to offer no control. However, sometimes a person's faith, religion, belief or spirituality can provide a sense of peace, acceptance and happiness – changing our perspective on a situation, even when taking control is not appropriate or achievable.

'Get a Life' needs audit scaling system: personal development

The scaling system in the table below applies for each section discussed in this chapter and is based on your personal perception of whether there is a deficiency, imbalance or need... or not. Everyone is different so there's no right or wrong. This simply allows you to consider the gaps that exist for you.

The scoring uses a self-rating percentage index from 0–100 with 0 per cent referring to needs totally **unmet** and 100 per cent equating to needs totally **met**. Add up the percentage totals and divide this by the number of sections to give you a total percentage for this chapter. At the end of the book, you will have a percentage total for each chapter, giving you scope to consider where you need to prioritize action.

If any sections are irrelevant to you, ignore them and reduce the number of sections you divide this by accordingly.

	Sections	Percentage of needs currently met %
1	Sufficient time for rest and relaxation	
2	Living in the moment and being mindful	
3	Accepting situations as they occur	
4	Expression of creativity	
5	Adventure and excitement	
6	Ability to manage life events	
7	Emotional intelligence	
8	Spirituality, religion, belief and faith	
Total Score for Chapter 1 (out of 800%): Personal Development		
Divide this Total Score by **8**		
Total Percentage Score (out of 100%) for Chapter 1		

For the more visually minded, plot a dot on the radar diagram below with the same percentage scale: 0 for needs totally unmet up to 100 per cent for needs totally met. You can then join the dots together to form a needs audit radar. This method gives you a visual cue to identify the gaps in your needs.

Personal development is concerned with a continual learning and rediscovery of ourselves and who we are becoming. Ebbs and flows will be influenced by work and personal life events and whilst we may not be able to control these, we can control how we respond and react to them.

Figure 1.1   Personal development needs audit radar

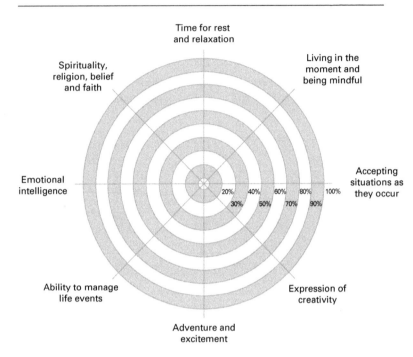

The next section looks at People and how our work–life balance is inextricably tied up by the relationships we have in our worlds.

02
People

Me, my partner and romance

Finding time for ourselves and our close relationships is central to building the right work–life balance for us.

Healthy and nourishing relationships contribute to our overall wellbeing and allow us to have a positive and uncluttered focus, both in work and in our personal life. The converse is that dysfunctional, damaging and disruptive personal relationships may distract us from our work, whilst fraught work-based relationships may cause us to brood and worry when we get home. Managing relationships at home and work is fundamental to a successful work–life balance because when they work well they become a crucial facilitator for this balance.

There's no optimal scheduling that's right or wrong for any relationship or an ideal degree of intensity or intimacy sought or expressed. We're all different, as are our needs. What's important is that we pay attention to our two-way relationship needs – our connection to others, and theirs to us – so we can ensure that sufficient time and effort is being engaged and this is not being ignored.

Being single

First, let's take being single. Everyone on this earth starts out as a single person and many very functional and happy people remain single for long periods of time, whether by choice or not. However, there's a common perception that the 'normal' way of life is to settle down with someone who's drop-dead gorgeous, will satisfy us all the time in every possible way, will never argue with or criticize us, will enjoy being with our families and friends, will earn a fortune but also spend masses of time with our beautiful and well-behaved kids. 'Society', including friends and family, often seems to infer that you can only be happy if you are in a relationship; that remaining single implies that there's some deficiency or confusion about sexual orientation.

Whilst both could be true, many people choose to prioritize themselves (they like the independence and autonomy of singledom), focus on their work (there's no space for a relationship), concentrate on their children (as busy single parents), pursue their aspirations (they haven't met the right person for them), stick with their memories (as widows and widowers), maintain their mental health (after past abusive relationships) and so on.

You probably need to be happy in yourself before you can give your best shot at a relationship. Being single gives us the perfect training ground to tussle with anchors from the past, allow us to become self-aware, emotionally intelligent and alert to the triggers of our stresses as well as learning how to build relationships with other people with empathy, compassion and appropriate assertiveness.

Fitting time in for our self includes much of what we've discussed in Chapter 1: learning about ourselves, developing personal skills and competencies and understanding how our needs and wants fit in with those of others. Chapter 5 addresses Psychological and Physical Wellbeing, so we'll cover self-care and coping skills later. But for this section it's about us in relationship with our selves, and in relationship with others.

We can have very close, engaged and committed relationships with others and remain single. Think back to some of your closest friendships and you'll resonate with the value of these connections. The question for the single person is the degree to which we remain single by choice or because we are prioritizing other aspects of our life.

Work can become an oasis of distraction to our personal relationships. We can feel needed and appreciated, even loved at work in a close parallel to a personal relationship. But some people get sucked into this distraction and after a number of years find that they are totally out of the relationship loop or the time-clock is changing priorities, particularly with having kids (if that is our choice). Again, the point is not to challenge being single. The challenge is to get us to consider our needs, which might involve staying single.

Should we decide to 'get out there' and seek the potential of a new personal relationship, the key is to manage perceptions and expectations.

If you don't know who you are (your needs, wants, hopes, dreams, beliefs, values, etc) how is anyone else going to get a fix on this? What sense are they going to make of you?

Nick

Nick had presented as anxious, depressed, fixated on how others saw him and starved of any sense of his own creativity, passion, drive and connectedness. He'd read many self-help books and had an external map of 'how to be', yet he had little sense of who he actually was. We worked on 'Who am I?', a tool I've evolved before, to map out a personal profile mosaic just for him, so he could start to see himself on paper and then integrate this into his sense of self.

Asking a set of 10 questions helped address these issues by focusing on what he had (albeit mostly hidden or denied), not what he didn't have.

Work–life balance action
The 'Who am I?' tool

The 'Who am I?' tool builds a personal profile mosaic tailored to each individual by asking some simple questions. For Nick, we crafted the following:

- What makes you laugh out loud on your own?
- What best contributes to your happiness?
- What do you think friends like about you most?
- How do you express yourself creatively and how often do you do this?
- What did you do last to help someone else and why?
- How do you best chill out and relax?
- Who most inspires you and why have you chosen this person?
- What are you most proud of and why?
- What excites you most in life and why?
- What do you like most about yourself and why?

Think about these questions, adding or removing any that may help you build your own personal profile mosaic.

I've seen many people over the years who have been drawn to the online dating world. Not only do we struggle with writing profiles that we believe make us sound worth meeting but even when we have done this it can be hard when we see the profiles of others: there always seems to be someone with better attributes than us. It's depressing. But it's life. Online dating certainly has its place when there may be a lack of meeting opportunities elsewhere but the advice is to caution against falling into the tick-box fantasy of seeking the perfect relationship. That's what online dating sites make their money from: chasing the dream. This is not to undersell yourself or discourage you from considering what's important to you in a relationship, rather it's about keeping a reality check in place.

Harry

Harry came to see me when he realized his drive to jump up the career path at his legal practice had alienated his need to be in a relationship. But his struggle was not about being ready for a relationship; it was more about the absolute fear and anxiety this generated within him. He was 'out of practice' and, as he put it, 'like a 13-year-old again'. He had no problem meeting people on various online dating sites, but he became paralysed as soon as he met someone he was attracted to. He was awash with all the negative 'selfs' – self-doubt, self-confidence, self-worth, self-criticism and so on.

What helped Harry was to go into each date with a tweaked mindset, one where he focused on building a connection, intrigue and interest in the other person, putting the spotlight on them, not him. In this way he suspended the fixation on how he might be regarded by those he met and it allowed him to be more himself: the chatty, engaging and affable person he was.

Humans are social creatures – we need to be in relationships, not least with ourselves. A big impediment to future relationships… is past relationships. I've worked with countless clients over the years who have escaped abusive relationships (psychological, physical or sexual) and each journey to recover and rejuvenate is unique and complex. The common theme, however, is the wish or need to make sense of what happened and to 'move on'. We can get anchored by former traumatic, abusive or manipulative relationships – whether this is a partner, or a boss or colleague at work. We can't control how someone might be or behave, nor can we change what's already happened, but we *can* have some control over how this affects us, and how we respond to moving on from situations for a better future. Although it's both common and natural to feel some guilt or blame associated with the actions of others (which can then hold us back at work and in the rest of our lives) – ultimately, we can't be responsible for those actions. We can only be responsible for ourselves.

Unhealthy relationships: help and support

Of course, not every unhealthy relationship is in the past. Although we have looked a little bit at how past relationships can be impediments to future relationships, the sad reality is that many people remain in difficult or abusive relationships, feeling trapped, lost or obligated at some level to stay put. We'll look at some ways to reflect on the health and balance in your relationship in a moment. But if you feel as if this describes your situation, I encourage you to reach out for support – to friends and family, to your work's employee assistance programme, to a trained therapist or counsellor, or to one of the dedicated services here:

- Samaritans – www.samaritans.org/
- Womensaid – www.womensaid.org.uk/
- Counselling Directory – www.counselling-directory.org.uk/
- Relate UK – /www.relate.org.uk/
- 7Cups – online relationship chat-room – www.7cups.com/relationship-advice-chat-room
- Relationships Australia – www.relationships.org.au

Getting into and maintaining a relationship

If we're in a romantic relationship, there is often a 'honeymoon' period, when everything smells of roses. We're excited, in love, the passion kicks in and we're in heaven. Hopefully much of this remains with us throughout our relationship. And equally hopefully, we learn to evolve and consolidate our relationship with the more normal and routine aspects of life. Relationships, perhaps somewhat obviously, involve at least two people, meaning there are at least two equal segments. Each has a 50 per cent responsibility for their side. An imbalance can occur when one is putting disproportionately more into it than the other. Sometimes this is necessary and appropriate for a short period of time. But if it becomes long-term, resentment, stress or apathy can creep in.

Juggling secondary relationships

With two people in relationships, we have two careers and two sets of parents, families and friends. There's a lot of juggling to be done, compromises to be made and additional relationships to nurture. In our work–life balance, we may need to factor in and find time for our partner's family and friends. We may have the opportunity to share in happy events, such as birthdays and celebrations. There may also be tough times, involving accidents, illness and traumatic events. Whilst we too may be emotionally affected when this happens to our partner's friends or family, we may need to find a way to support our partner too.

Holidays

Whether it's for a long weekend or our annual vacation, holidays can be source of tension regarding families and friends. Do they join us or not? Does this involve your family and friends or theirs? Is there an imbalance on seeing one set of friends and family and not the others? Do we see them enough, or maybe we see them too much and want a break from them?

Reflecting on this and discussing it with your partner is important because holidays play a significant part in work–life balance: they represent a chance for us to recharge our batteries and have a well-deserved break from work routines. However, if they involve stressful family gatherings or conflicts with others, then we're likely to be screaming out to return to work.

Settling down

When we become more established in our relationship, it's often referred to as 'settling down'. The problem with this term is that it suggests there comes a time when we just get into a pattern or routine and simply get on with our lives. Relationships are more like plants – roses even. We need to nurture, feed and pay attention to them or they can deteriorate, or even come back and bite us like a Venus flytrap.

As Andrew and Sally found on the Greece holiday referred to in Chapter 1, personal needs change and the balance in the relationship requires tweaking. Compromises do have to be made. If it's all one-way, it's imbalanced. Some relationships do operate in this way, and perfectly well, because it has been communicated and agreed in advance. These situations are less about imbalance and more about distinctive roles and responsibilities.

Ken and Laura

Ken and Laura experienced several careers, where Ken was a freelance musician whilst Laura brought up their kids. Ken then retrained as a teacher and later became a headmaster. Laura supported him in this second role as the 'headmaster's wife', taking on duties that supported Ken's role. Both agreed, planned and worked with these defined roles to support one another. This was the way of their relationship. It might not work for everyone, but it worked for them.

What both couples achieved was a way to understand how their relationship operated from their combined engines. But it does take effort and attention. As part of our successful work–life balance, this is certainly one area that benefits from consideration.

One of the tools I developed to help clients reflect on their relationships is a Relationship Audit model. This evolved when I ran a relationship coaching consultancy in the 1990s. A comparable but different version of this has been published elsewhere.[1]

For any stage of a relationship, it can help as part of our work–life balance to establish the current situation: where we are at, what needs fixing now and what may need attention soon. Here is an exercise to try.

Work–life balance action
Relationship audit

The relationship audit is intended to be completed individually but the results shared and discussed between the two of you. Add a few extra questions which you think need to be asked of your relationship:

- What are the five most important attributes you love about your partner?
- What do you take for granted in your partner?
- How do you spend quality time with your partner?
- When do you most enjoy being with your partner?
- What are the things which most irritate you about your partner?
- How and when do you demonstrate your love for your partner?
- How can you improve your sexual relationship with your partner?
- How do children, friends and family impact your relationship (positively and negatively)?
- How can you improve communication and understanding in your relationship?
- To what extent does your relationship fit into your work–life balance?
- How can you better support and encourage your partner?
- What future events might challenge or impact your relationship?
- What is the one thing you can say or do to improve your relationship?

Whilst a relationship audit is presented here to focus on our closer and more personal relationships, it may also be prudent to ponder the positives and negatives in work-related relationships too, perhaps without the more intimate questions. Both have a comparable impact on work–life balance in that they can operate smoothly in isolation or create distracting angst and stress.

Break-ups

What about when romantic relationships come to an end? Well, it's worth mentioning that a relationship break-up can be devastating. It can feel like a bereavement, affecting the core of who we are and our very existence. Time needs to be given to work through this. Throwing ourselves into work might help for some people; but for others it is necessary to take a step back, regroup, recharge batteries and take personal care. This needs to be factored with some leverage into our current work–life balance. Taking time out might be needed, seeking counsel with people who can offer you what you need.

Demands and needs of children

Every parent aspires to be a perfect parent. We start out with the intent of being the best of the best... and usually end up seeking mere survival! The secret is about being 'good enough'. This is more real and achievable.

Quite how anyone creates a successful work–life balance when juggling the demands of children is almost a mystery – and yet it can be done. Like so many aspects of work–life balance, we will each have our own complex matrix of variables, resources and opportunities which will impact this. Some may be able to free up time with access to childcare, or utilize the support of willing and able family members, and so on. Or we may be lumbered with a partner who at best is non-responsive and at worst absorbs our time like an additional child. Or we may be a single parent and need to balance a confetti-shower of roles and responsibilities. It's never easy.

It's often helpful to differentiate what might be *our* needs from those of our children, as these may differ or conflict. Children might look and behave like 'mini-mes' but they're still kids. They need love, nurturing, guidance, structure, advice, support, education, inspiration, routine, praise, motivation, encouragement... it just goes on and on and it can change moment by moment. In one situation they may need empathic acknowledgement and sympathy; in others, it will be discipline and boundaries. Whether we are in a paid job, or work as a parent, we'll need to find the time to meet the different needs throughout our offspring's childhoods.

Larry

Early childhood for Larry appeared to be full of family fun. With two brothers, there was always plenty to do, games to play and activities to enjoy. He presented to me with intense perfectionism traits: he'd felt the need to achieve the best grades, be happy all the time, deal with struggles perfectly and essentially be a model human. His reality reflected the myth of perfectionism – it's impossible and it creates a continual negative spiral of incompleteness. Larry felt that his older brother was always expected to be the 'sensible one', and treated by their parents (in Larry's view) as wise and mature. The youngest sibling was the 'baby' so given – again, as far as Larry was concerned – special attention. Larry felt largely ignored and this forged his need to be perfect, prove himself and 'shine'.

But it needs to work both ways. Parents and carers need time off too, and may feel pulled in all directions by children's needs. It's about getting a balance which suits us all, acknowledging that if we don't take time to relax and refresh, we'll burn out and won't be much use to our kids. 'Negotiation with perspiration' was how a friend of mine defined parenting. We all want an easy life but sometimes we can make things difficult for ourselves or generate stress where this isn't necessary. Perhaps we don't need to win every battle. Maybe we need to admit our mistakes when we get something wrong.

Playtime

Planning fun, stimulating or engaging activities can help a child's development. This might involve ferrying them around to after-school sports, guides/scouts, drama/dance classes or any of a huge number of options: whoever invented the 'Dad's Taxi' stickers has probably retired to the Maldives. There's also much we can do ourselves including days out to the beach or to museums, or even just playing board games indoors. It's about making the time for the relationship and allowing the child to develop, learn and grow (in all senses).

There needs to be a degree of mutuality about playtime, so it's not all directed at the children. It may be about an activity that is pitched at the child's level but that shouldn't prevent us enjoying it too. Perhaps there are family events and activities which we'll all enjoy, such as a trip to a pantomime or a walk in the country. Additionally, we might have a hobby or interest which our children could learn to understand and appreciate. If we are enjoying, satisfying or nourishing ourselves, it might be easier to encourage an interest and engagement for the young ones too.

My father used to play golf and from an early age encouraged me to join him. After a few basic lessons which taught me which way up to hold a club, I would accompany him to our local municipal course. I found the experience thoroughly enjoyable and highly entertaining but perhaps not for the reasons he intended. A frequent slicer of golf shots, my father would sometimes reach such a peak of rage that he would frustratingly fling his golf club further than he had hit the ball.

Regrettably, I doubt whether my father experienced golf as a positive work–life balance activity.

Family structure and routine

There's often an oasis of calm and peace when they get to school as that might give six hours or so when we can get on with our lives but before and after we will be back in demand again. It's often helpful to devise a family schedule setting out who's doing what, where and when... and possibly why. This will no doubt change weekly (if not daily) but at least it creates a plan to work around.

Work–life balance action
Creating a family schedule

Table 2.1 is a template for a family schedule for you to fill in. You might add in other regular categories or assign tasks to different members of the family, ie a 'global' chart including everyone or one each.

Emotional development and resilience

A significant part of nurturing a child's development is allowing them to forge a degree of independence and autonomy to make their own decisions and learn about risk and responsibility. We develop resilience and a capacity to cope with difficult situations through life experience. Exposing children to managed and appropriate risk and responsibility gives them experience of dealing with different situations with a range of possible outcomes or consequences. As this book journeys through a work–life balance, the same balance is pertinent to how we mediate risk and responsibility for our children.

We all need to be able to deal with disappointment, loss and rejection. It's not nice but it happens, and isolating ourselves from difficult situations doesn't make them go away. How we respond or react to difficult situations can have the effect of being modelled

Table 2.1 Family schedule

Date	Monday	Tuesday	Wednesday	Thursday	Friday	Saturday	Sunday
School priorities							
After-school activities							
Family time							
Help at home							
Evenings							
Work or community							
Shopping							
Other stuff							

by our children. They can learn from our ability to cope and, conversely, pick up bad habits that come from us. If we jump into a pit of depression when we experience a disappointment, it's possible this may be interpreted by our children as 'the way' to behave in such situations. Alternatively, if we have the ability to recognize the disappointment and bounce back from it, this may become learnt behaviour for the children.

As we discussed in Chapter 1, a lot of people say they don't like confrontation, when in fact what they're saying is that they haven't learnt to effectively deal with hostile, aggressive or anger-laden situations. This is very much part of work–life balance because it reflects the fact that the time invested in managing a situation appropriately saves much more time than picking up the pieces of something we handled badly.

Boundaries

An additional ingredient in creating a successful work–life balance is the ability for us to create boundaries. Not only does this offer a degree of protection and emotional space for us but it creates much-needed structure and guidance for our children. With boundaries comes discipline. When parenting with someone else, the key is knowing, sharing and maintaining the same boundaries.

For every parent, there's one word associated with children which strikes abject fear… hormones. This 'H' word accounts for one of the most uncontrollable aspects of parenting. As our children grow and hit puberty the hormones kick in with alarming confusion and uncertainty. It becomes a bit like juggling lumps of butter: things can get messy pretty quickly. It becomes impossible to make sufficient preparation as the unpredictability of moods and emotions run amok. All we can do is build in some time and space for volatile eruptions, believing and hoping calmness will prevail again soon.

Whatever age, children need appropriate boundaries even if they challenge us, react and push against them. That's all part of learning what boundaries are and why they exist. It can be difficult to say 'no' and we might not be thanked for it, but 'no' is a crucial boundary word. The second most crucial boundary word is 'because', so we give some reason, context and rationale. This all becomes part of our work–life balance as we structure our life around the time and re-sources available to us. Saying 'yes' to everything is impossible.

We have all been parented in some shape or form and this will in-fluence our own attitude and perspective on what we do. Whether this has been positive or negative, it's useful to reflect on the impact it has had on us so we can learn from or guard against any unhelpful traits.

If our parents are still in our lives, they can certainly offer a rich potential to our work–life balancing as they may help fill in the gaps that our work might restrict or prevent.

However, there may be tensions surrounding 'who knows best'. It's more realistic to recognize that there will be times that they will be a great asset to us and other times they may hinder. What will help here is open communication and transparency, giving appre-ciation where deserved or asserting our priorities when needed. Whilst considering boundaries for our children, we may need to negotiate a similar strategy for our parents.

Child-less or child-free

It's important to acknowledge that not everyone has or wants chil-dren. There can be a lot of pressure for those child-less or 'child-free' to sometimes compensate for those with children. Employees at work who have children might stampede for holiday leave enti-tlement during school holidays, assuming it will be OK for those without children to accept different leave periods. For those with-out children, there's a different perspective on work–life balance and the challenge of using the time when others might be engaged with their own children. It isn't the job of this book to tell anyone what to do; rather it's encouraging us to reflect on the savvy use of the time we have and the demands on us.

Not having children, whether by choice or not, certainly changes the framework and matrix of our work–life balance. There may be different choices and opportunities available for people who have children and those who do not. It's up to us how we want to fill our lives and find the nourishment and life satisfaction we deserve.

For those who do not have children and this is not through choice, ie fertility issues, trauma etc, this may represent an emotionally sensitive area and one where external therapeutic support could be of benefit. Please see the available resources in the Appendix for more information.

Friends

It is said that you can choose your friends but not your family. Of course, for many, that's not quite true. When we're at school, further education or at work, we may not have much choice over the people we interact with, and the extent to which we want to be friends with them or not.

In our early years, friends become a key part of early peer socialization as we learn to modulate and moderate how we fit in to various groups or not, and importantly, what needs are met in the process. The pressure to fit in is huge, and we can feel traumatized if we get isolated or ostracized. Social media has had a significant impact upon this with its implied quest to compete for the number of friends we have, the 'likes' we get, or the degree of fun and excitement we 'should' be experiencing.

Friendships often emerge because of things we have in common, particularly through education, work or non-work activities such as sport. These shared interests can create a strong social glue. The key thing to consider is not so much who our friends are or the quantity of them, but rather the quality of our friendship; how are the mutual friendship needs being met? How many of us have experienced the 'friend' who's always running to us in a crisis or asks us for a favour, yet when the tables are turned they're nowhere to be seen? There needs to be a mutuality, a reciprocity. This is big when it comes to work–life balance. Social networks beyond work and family can help maintain it, but it also helps ensure that one-sidedness in any relationship doesn't become the norm or expectation.

Mohammed

After the death of his mother, Mohammed found himself reappraising his values and in so doing started to reassess who he was friends with and why. Many of his friends were from his early childhood or had emerged through the course of life stages, including school, college and work. The bereavement triggered him to reflect on his life and relationships, and he realized that some of his friendships were probably holding him back or were dysfunctional or destructive. In particular, he found that he no longer enjoyed the persistently regular visits to the pub that they all sought, or the conversations they had. Whilst reinforcing his few truly real and close friends he chose to cut ties with those he felt were not good for him.

Alongside this, just like for any relationship, we need to put equal effort and time into our friendships. We might have 500+ friends on Facebook… but how many have we spoken to recently? Sometimes it can be affirming to simply message to say 'hello' to someone you haven't spoken to for a while or actually say 'you're a good friend'. However, be wary of straying into 'you're my bestest bestest friend' territory as this can put undue pressure on the friendship. It's not to say we shouldn't have a best friend – but why limit it to one?

Family

When it comes to family, we'll all have our unique framework and network, and with the growing interest surrounding genealogy and ancestry, more people are choosing to widen their family circle further by building relationships with newly discovered relatives.

Like with friends, we need to put the time in to nurture or manage these relationships. They might be warm, affectionate and connecting or they could be fractious, argumentative and toxic. There's no clear pathway in terms of how to best get on with our family but it's important to have an empathic awareness of the dynamics, social scripts and traits which might exist.

Some extended families operate through togetherness and connection; for others, connections may be upheld more by feelings of obligation and necessity. We've probably all got at least one relative whose pending visit strikes doom or dread in us, but another whom we undervalue and under-appreciate. Do we need to make a conscious effort to see more of our family or even less? Though we share a bloodline, we're still different individuals: we're not necessarily like them and they're not necessarily like us.

The life-long connection we have to families means there are bound to be triggers or flashpoints along the way based on things that were said or done or not said and not done. People can harbour grudges, including us. If not acknowledged, managed or resolved, they can consume a huge amount of distracted time. Compromises might need to be made along the way, including acknowledgements that it's best to simply agree to disagree on particular topics or discussion points.

On 18 September 2014 there was a referendum in Scotland for independence from the United Kingdom. As it happened, 55 per cent voted against it and 45 per cent voted for it. During all the campaigning, there was a passionate debate on both sides. Results suggest that younger people voted 'for' as a change and for a different future, whereas older people tended to vote 'against' in favour of the status quo. Family members often found themselves strongly disagreeing with each other and the battle lines were drawn. Even six years on, there are few Scottish families unaffected by what happened.

As we tussle with 'family' in our work–life balance, clearly there becomes a focus on nurturing, appreciating and growing the good and positive relationships we have whilst also considering whether we need to distance ourselves from the ones which sap our time, strength and energy. That's not to say we shouldn't build bridges where the tides have washed them away; rather we should be circumspect and realistic, putting in the time and effort we can, when and where appropriate.

Even in our seemingly hyper-connected societies, many family networks are struggling to simply keep in touch. Family can be important to us at any stage of our life. The elderly relatives might feel isolated as much as the younger ones as each group struggles with their own life stages and the challenges these bring. Just because someone might be our second cousin once removed doesn't diminish the impact we could have on their lives and vice versa.

At the time of writing, Brexit is swamping the media airwaves as the United Kingdom struggles to make up its mind about its relationship with Europe. I was reminded by a relative of mine recently that my grandmother on my mother's side, who died when I was very young, was actually born in Madeira. Not only did this add further impetus to my quest to learn Portuguese but it opened up a potential route for me to retain some European connection if the UK really does 'leave'. If my late grandmother was alive today I'd say to her *Ola, duas cervejas por favor*. OK, other than some essential stock phrases, my Portuguese vocabulary needs a lot of improvement.

Niamh

Belonging to a large family in south-west Ireland, Niamh had reached a stuck point in her career where she didn't seem to be able to locate any obvious appropriate promotional opportunities in her accountancy firm in Edinburgh. She was successful and a corporate partner, the point she had always told her parents she'd reach. She came to me because she had hit a career wall: the shine seemed to have come off because, in her eyes, she had nothing left to achieve. I could see her enthusiasm for what she'd done and part of her didn't want to throw it away. After some soul searching and personal values exploration, she elected to return to Ireland and set up as a freelance book-keeper in a town near her family. The letter I received from her some time later confirmed she had found what she had been looking for: a less pressured job close to people she loved.

Whether we want to see more or less of our extended family, the point is that we need to plot this into our work–life balance matrix.

Pets and animals

Whilst pets and animals are not strictly speaking people, they do constitute a potentially rich source of a work–life balance. As well as the more traditional pets of dogs, horses and cats, guinea pigs and rabbits, I've known other more unusual pets which are adored by their owners: pot-bellied pigs, llamas, snakes and reptiles, chickens and so on.

Most animals considered pets will require our time and effort to look after their health and wellbeing, and some would argue that we derive a similar value as a result, whether this is 'walkies' first thing in the morning or last thing at night, or the sheer enjoyment we generate from their response to us as their 'keeper'. Research published in Nature.com claimed that dogs can help reduce cardiovascular risk in their owners by providing social support and motivation for physical activity.[2] The companionship of pets or animals can also create an opportunity to bond with another and provide support, nurturing and love.

About 20 years ago, I hosted a mini-aquarium of exotic fish in my therapy room until this became such a distraction to gawping clients that I felt obliged to pass it on. However, it did create an oasis of relaxation: one client asked at the beginning of the session if he could just sit and watch the fish for an hour. Whilst he could have done something similar at the local pet shop for free it reflected the mindful and peaceful serenity that some people derive from animals.

Jacob

It was a 'double whammy', as Jacob put it, when he lost his beloved grandmother and his pet dog Dougal within days of each other. His grandmother had been unwell for some time, so her passing was anticipated in the near future. Dougal's, however, was completely unexpected. His relationship with Dougal had also been much more mutually dependent. For the best part of five years, Jacob had fed and groomed him, walked him twice a day and worried about him when he was ill. Jacob presented not with the accumulation of losses or bereavement per se, rather the guilt associated with feeling more bereft from his dog's passing than his grandmother's. When he brought in two mementos of them both to one of our sessions, it wasn't the photo of his grandmother that affected him most; it was Dougal's toy rubber chicken.

In my university, we provide 'therapets' at pinch-points in the academic calendar, particularly before exams. This creates a time and a space for students to enjoy a bit of time-out with a cute, fluffy pet. Many tell us it reminds them of home or of a past positive experience with someone they knew who owned a dog. These therapets are specially trained and usually with a known calm temperament. But many of their owners offer this service for free because they love the reaction and response from students.

Contribution to community

Society would cease to function if there was no sense of community. We are all part of a social grouping based on some form of commonality or shared living space; from street to town to region to nation. We all want to belong to, and be connected with, where we live. Getting connected to our locality requires action on our part. We need to get out and do something. Helping others is one of the best ways of achieving this. It's also a great antidote to work and can contribute to a significant feel-good factor in our work–life balance.

How many of us do you think are involved in volunteering – you, your family, friends, work colleagues? It's much more than most of us would think. In the UK in 2015, around 42 per cent of the population were involved in some form of volunteering, rising to 58 per cent for students, whilst volunteering through a formal organization was valued in 2014 at £23 billion even without the smaller-scale opportunities not associated with established charities.[3] Amongst many other reputable volunteering bodies, the Do It Foundation is a UK-based organization that claims to host approximately a million volunteering opportunities in the UK. The scale and scope of volunteering is massive.

People who volunteer do so because they enjoy meeting and helping others, gaining new or using existing skills and benefiting from the experience. It doesn't have to be a huge time contribution or effort. It can simply be chipping in the spare time when we can. Whether it's befriending, ferrying people to a hospital appointment, helping out with lunches, organizing a youth sports event, supporting a community centre or joining a phoneline, there are loads of volunteering options.

Our location, family life-stage, affluence, connections and personal needs will all contribute to identifying the opportunities that might abound for us. If we have pre-teen children, this might sway us to organize children's sporting events or outdoor activities because our children might be part of this too. If we are retired we might wish to stave off isolation by volunteering in a charity shop, or offering tutoring to those who need it. If we are part of a church or religious group we may enjoy offering our time in support of these communities because of the shared faith or belief.

The question is not so much *where* to volunteer... but *why not* volunteer? It's not a life-long commitment, yet the benefits could be. It may not seem likely initially, but there are probably many opportunities available to support your local community. It may not pay directly but the wider benefits of your input can be far-reaching, and you'll realize the intense 'feel-good' vibes which can ooze from it.

Vanessa

After many years climbing the corporate ladder, Vanessa reached the heights of director of human resources for her educational institution. But in doing so she started to feel there was more to life that the role she'd achieved. We audited her needs and wants and after negotiating her hours with her employer, she reduced her full-time role to four days a week and joined a cancer charity driving people to and from hospice events. Whilst I believe these cancer survivors will have enjoyed her friendly banter, I think a degree of enthusiasm for being escorted by her was also associated with her plush, top-of-the-range Mercedes. They'd joke about her being their chauffeur.

Volunteering doesn't require us to have a Mercedes, though as Vanessa found, it can help.

As our population ages and respective healthcare systems creak under increased demand and reduced resources, more and more of us are providing personal and supportive care for our friends and relatives alongside our other responsibilities. In the UK, according to Carers UK research in 2015, one in eight (6.5 million) adults were carers and this is expected to rise to 9 million by 2037. Over 3 million people juggle care with work.[4]

Caring ranges from keeping someone company and doing their meals, shopping or laundry through to personal care and physical help. It can range from short periods of time to live-in full-time.

From a work–life balance perspective, with volunteering and caring responsibilities, it's important to consider the needs that exist, and our capacity to schedule, prioritize and determine what's important in our lives.

Relationships at work

There are many conscious and sub-conscious dynamics which come into play with work relationships. Unless it's a start-up organization, we'll be coming into a team that already exists. Hopefully they'll welcome us with open arms and enthusiastically help us to find our feet and adjust to our new role. But there will also be an element of uncertainty, and in some cases mistrust. Are we going to fit in and join in or might we be a part of change or schism that they might resist? Sometimes it helps to ease in by slipping under the group radar, rather than going in with guns blazing.

How we adapt and connect with work colleagues depends on our personality, characteristics, behaviours and job roles – and theirs. There may be a hierarchy in place, or it could be a flatter structure. Getting to know the cultural norms, explicit and implicit, is an ongoing challenge as they can change and adapt based on workplace demands. We can learn by what we see and hear. What is the tone, content and context of professionalism? If there is a degree of banter or humour, to what extent does this help or hinder professionalism? Even matching the dress code will speak volumes for how others will connect with us.

Asking for help, advice or assistance shows we are keen to do our job well and that we trust the expertise of others. Sometimes it's difficult to know what questions we need to ask or how to pitch them to the most appropriate person at the right time. We might feel we 'should' know the answers or what to do, but everyone comes from a place of ignorance or uncertainty until they build up knowledge, expertise and experience.

Effective and enjoyable working relationships make a huge difference to our experience of life at work. It boosts our confidence in collaborative working, it allows us to delegate more easily and we feel the synergistic benefits of team-working. Good working relationships enable a team to thrive and blossom. Even when working on our own tasks, we know there may be others out there with whom we can connect. It might seem a bit obvious but we all want to work with people we enjoy working with. We have some responsibility in this to become an enjoyable person to work with.

However, we're not always going to get on with everyone we work with, though we should maintain professionalism in our relationships with them.

Problems often occur when one person's needs conflict with another's, whether this is personal, professional or a blend of the two. The key to managing this is to appreciate the 'needs' focus and direction. Is the tension about our needs or theirs? Fear of change or the unknown is a further conflict trigger. Most of us like to feel knowledgeable. We don't like the unknown because we don't know the potential consequences and how it might affect us.

We'd all like to say that we aim to treat people the way we would want to be treated ourselves. Yet in the heat of the moment, with deadlines whizzing past, tensions growing and stress oozing out of our pores, we often lose sight of this. Tense situations can be dealt with more effectively and sensitively if we simply take a moment to 'step back', draw a deep breath, even count to 10, before saying something. Remaining cool, calm and collected works better than a hot-headed, firing-from-the-hip approach.

Salma

Following tension at her work, Salma presented to me with a frustration that she didn't 'match' the pace of conversation or interaction with colleagues. She was self-critical of what she regarded as her 'introversion' against a culture of 'extroversion'. As we modelled and explored different ways of communication within the sphere of her character and personality, she started to recognize that she couldn't get away from the fact that indeed she was quieter than others. But, and this was the pivotal 'but', she recognized that precisely because she was quieter, others would listen to her more intensely. She didn't need to change anything about her. She just needed to appreciate the way she was.

Conflict at work

As I've mentioned in previous sections, many of us say we fear conflict when we often mean we haven't effectively learnt to disagree constructively with another person. We shy away from a perceived threat of explosive aggression which further prevents us facing the fear. Facing our anxiety will often help us respond to, deal with and resolve the threat in an appropriate way: it can be a conversation, not a battle, with the other person. If we own the impact on us, we side-step judgement and criticism of the other person which immediately deflates the tension.

Liggy and Beryl

I provided a short mediation meeting between Liggy and Beryl. They'd had a massive shouting match at work over their different interpretations of the annual leave policy. I asked them individually to separate facts and emotion. They pretty much agreed on both. The facts centred on a poorly worded leave policy. Their emotions focused on their respective family holiday needs and how these felt ignored by the other. Within about 30 minutes, they agreed to constructively seek clarification from their human resources department, and had come to appreciate that they shared similar family holiday needs. Game, set, match.

In many cases we simply do not have all the facts to make a reasoned assessment of a situation, which makes it easier to take something personally, and occasionally incorrectly. Though we may not feel comfortable sharing personal situations or concerns with colleagues, what happens outside of work can impact upon it.

If our colleague is snappy or argumentative, are we aware they're struggling with their mortgage, or an infirm elderly parent, or a baby that was screaming all last night, or a difficult relationship, or an alcohol addiction, or a fear of redundancy and so on? Probably not. Compassion and empathy resolve a lot of problems.

As we seek to better understand others, we need to understand our own behaviours and habits. Do we inadvertently feed the potential for difficult relationships? I remember from an early age, my father warned me that 'he who gossips with you, gossips of you'. I think I was about seven years old at the time so didn't really understand it but later in life I found this to be very true. It's best to avoid gossiping about and with others at all: it serves nothing or no one and usually comes swinging back to nip us on the toes.

We might have the patience of a saint and the negotiation skills of a UN diplomat and yet still find ourselves mired in a troublesome work relationship. Ideally, we'd be able to meet with the cause of the problem, sort things out and then shake hands and make up. Or, we'll need to elevate this to a boss or manager. However, it may be that a formal process is required. With any fractious situation, often it helps to clarify how we want something resolved. Do we want an apology, something to change, a shared empathic awareness or a clarity of understanding?

Grievance and disciplinary policies exist at work precisely because human behaviour means some people will stray off the organizational reservation. This can be stressful for all concerned so it is worth seeking advice and identifying support resources available.

Networking and your dream team

We want positive and productive relationships with our colleagues at work, so the work starts today either patching up the damaged ones or nurturing the new ones. There's a big world out there in terms of the number of potential working contacts but it's actually quite a small world when it comes down to the circle of people directly connected to our work lives. (Unless you're someone like Jackie Stewart…!)

A lot of people shy away from 'networking' because it conjures up an image of a glossy salesperson in a shiny suit with perfect pearl-white teeth and a smile the size of a letter box. Others have this misunderstood view that networking is about exploiting other people. Networking, though, is simply about making contact with others, finding opportunities to develop real and genuine relationships.

It needs to be a two-way process to operate effectively. We help them and they'll help us. An imbalance will simply alienate one from the other and the contact will dissolve. Many of us don't like to ask for help, advice or guidance, preferring to wait for things to sort out or run their course. Often, this strategy means that nothing moves.

Networking becomes a further spoke to our work–life balance wheel because it's about identifying and sharing timely, useful and relevant learning, information and insight. I like it because it's a sort of social delegation by sharing the load. Online networks proliferate today because of their huge potential reach but the face-to-face method still offers the best personal touch. A combination of both is probably ideal.

Liz

I worked with Liz about 20 years ago in the employee assistance profession and then our paths parted only to be rekindled about six months ago. I was delighted when she contacted me out of the blue via an online business community to congratulate me on the publication of my previous book. During our e-mail exchanges, we shared a mutual appreciation over what we had done over the prior decades both personally and professionally. In doing so, she identified an Australian contact of hers who she thought might be helpful for me on a topic of mutual interest. I was very grateful for this opportunity to connect. And then no contact for three months until Liz got back in touch with me to let me know of the Change-Transitions workshop she was running. As I could think of many who would find this of interest, I was happy to promote this throughout my online network. That's networking.

We all need to sell or pitch ourselves when we're involved in networking opportunities. Think of the interview situation. We want to demonstrate why we're the ideal candidate but we're also vetting the interviewers... do we really want to work for them or their organization?

> ## Work–life balance action
> The kettle pitch
>
> The kettle pitch is named to reflect the short time we might spend with someone in the office kitchen waiting for the kettle to boil. You have a short period of time to pitch yourself. Consider how you might describe your key attributes in three minutes to a university professor, a store check-out assistant and the golfing legend Tiger Woods. Why Tiger Woods? No reason. Just think of three very different people. You want them to raise their eyebrows with intrigue about you. You need a verbal script about you which is: 1) unique, 2) relevant and 3) memorable. If you forget these three tasks, just remember it needs to be memorable.

Successful work–life balance involves using our limited time wisely. The kettle pitch is one such example where we get straight to the point, quickly and decisively.

A number of years ago, I was on an interview panel. The candidates all knew we had a script of 14 key questions and an hour for the meeting. Some interviewees gave multiple or overly elaborate responses. The person who got the job nailed each question clearly, distinctively and succinctly. That particular interview finished early.

I mention this example because even when we get to the job interview stage, we're still effectively networking. We're pitching ourselves for a job but we're also building relationships with the people who have the power to employ us and with whom we may end up working.

The point about networking is to enable others to be our spokespeople and share the load of getting us, our attributes and our name out there. They could be our 'champions' in certain situations. The world revolves around social connections and this chapter serves to illustrate the value in people relationships. As we'll cover in more detail in Chapter 5 on Psychological and Physical Wellbeing, sometimes we can't do everything on our own. We need to reach out and ask for help and assistance.

A Dream Team is a term to describe the best possible combination of people gathered together for a particular purpose. It can be used in any of a number of contexts. In networking and work-related contacts, it represents the opportunity to pull in the many people we know who could favourably influence job development or career advancement.

Work–life balance action
Gathering a dream team

Think of a particular goal or purpose which might benefit by gathering a dream team of people around you who can contribute towards you achieving that objective. Think as laterally as you can. The goals could be made up from any of the topics in this book, eg

Figure 2.1 Your dream team

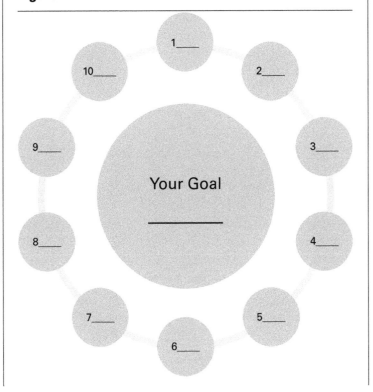

'Get and stay fit', 'Get a promotion', 'Make new friends', 'Time management improvement', 'Stress management' and so on. Write down the names of 10 people who could impact your goal. Depending on your goal, this might include your yoga buddy, golfing partner, therapist, neighbour, car-share friend, second cousin twice-removed, etc. You never know what nuggets of gold they could dig up for you.

For each member of your dream team, and in collaboration with them, you need to assign roles and responsibilities. What will they do when, where and how? Give them a brief, make it like a contract and allow them to share in the benefits you derive from their involvement.

The secret of effective networking is about broadening your networking landscape as much as possible, rather than just the obvious. We can never be sure who knows someone of influence who might have a positive influence on our world.

Sharon

Having worked hard on a three-year change strategy for her pharmaceutical sales team, Sharon felt she had concluded what she set out to achieve and needed a new challenge. We worked on developing her dream team to consider the spectrum of people and contacts she knew who might influence new opportunities. Whilst we included the 'usual' work-related contacts, we used some lateral thinking to identify 'people of influence' who were not work-related. Sharon was close to her sister and they both inspired and influenced each other. Shortly after, her sister got to know a human resources manager at antenatal classes and through a flurry of introductions, Sharon landed a cracking interview for a senior post in the NHS. The last I heard from her was that she was embarking on a monumental change strategy for an NHS Trust and was loving it. In Sharon's case, it was her sister who did the hard work, albeit whilst lying on cushions and focusing on deep breathing exercises.

Networking is most fun when we feel we have made a difference for someone and forged the unique connections that perhaps only we could have engineered. The more we help others, the more they help others too. It becomes a domino effect of helping heroes.

I tried an experiment recently. As I leave work, there's usually a slow crawl along a one-mile stretch of road, with traffic joining from a few side roads. Many times, if the traffic is moving, we ignore the vehicles trying to join the pace, pretending we haven't seen them. But if you let someone into the space in front of you, after being ignored by others ahead, you'll find their appreciation often makes them reciprocate and they too will let someone into the space in front of them. The slightly frustrating aspect of this is that your hospitable and kind act of letting one vehicle move in front of you may trigger 20 more! Try it.

'Get a Life' needs audit scaling system: people

The scaling system in the table below applies for each section discussed in this chapter and is based on your personal perception of whether there is a deficiency, imbalance or need... or not. Everyone is different so there's no right or wrong. This simply allows you to consider the gaps that exist for you.

The scoring uses a self-rating percentage index from 0–100 with 0 per cent referring to needs totally **unmet** and 100 per cent equating to needs totally **met**. Add up the percentage totals and divide this by the number of sections to give you a total percentage for this chapter. At the end of the book, you will have a percentage total for each chapter in the book, giving you scope to consider where you need to prioritize action.

If any sections are irrelevant to you, ignore them and reduce the number of sections you divide this by accordingly.

For the more visually minded, plot a dot on the radar diagram in Figure 2.2 with the same percentage scale: 0 for needs totally

	Sections	Percentage of needs currently met %
1	Me, my partner and romance	
2	Demands and needs of children	
3	Friends	
4	Family	
5	Pets and animals	
6	Contribution to community	
7	Relationships at work	
8	Networking and your dream team	
Total Score for Chapter 2 (out of 800%): People		
Divide this Total Score by **8**		
Total Percentage Score (out of 100%) for Chapter 2		

Figure 2.2   People needs audit radar

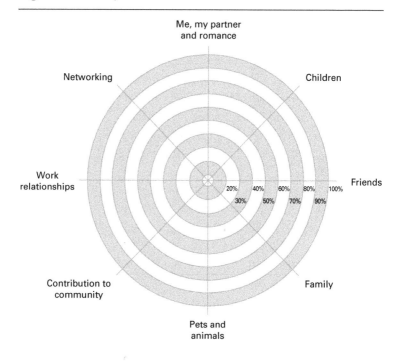

unmet up to 100 per cent for needs totally met. You can then join the dots together to form a needs audit radar. This method gives you a visual cue to identify the gaps in your needs.

'People' involves the crucial relationships we have and make with those we meet, live or work with in our world. Relationships come and go. They can blossom and develop or fracture and end. Ultimately it's up to us how we view and value people in our lives and how this contributes to our successful work–life balance.

The next chapter looks at Professional issues and the essential aspects of how we act, behave and get on in our life at work.

Endnotes

1 Hughes, RM, Kinder, A and Cooper, C (2019) *The Wellbeing Workout: How to manage stress and develop resilience*, Palgrave Macmillan, London

2 Mubanga, M, Byberg, L, Nowak, C, Egenvall, A, Magnusson, PK, Ingelsson, E and Fall, T (2017) Dog ownership and the risk of cardiovascular disease and death: a nationwide cohort study, *Scientific Reports*, 17 November. Available at: www.nature.com/articles/ s41598-017-16118-6 (archived at https://perma.cc/7H46-HX63)

3 Office for National Statistics (2017) *Changes in the value and division of unpaid volunteering in the UK: 2000 to 2015*, Office for National Statistics, London, 16 March. Available at: www.ons.gov.uk/economy/ nationalaccounts/satelliteaccounts/articles/changesinthevalueand divisionofunpaidcareworkintheuk/2015 (archived at https://perma.cc/ WQ6Y-G2CR)

4 Carers UK (2019) *Facts and Figures*. Available at: www.carersuk.org/ news-and-campaigns/press-releases/facts-and-figures (archived at https://perma.cc/6BUQ-Z2GN)

03
Professional issues

This chapter focuses on the professional dimension at work in a more macro sense – a sort of *why* we work. In Chapter 4, we will move on to look at Productivity and Performance, where we will delve deeper into the more micro intricacies of *how* we work.

Purpose and meaning at work

Why do we work? Why does anyone work? Why not laze around all day watching box-sets of dramas on Netflix or munching on long lunches in fancy cafés or lying in the sun sipping mojitos until we sizzle? Partly, and somewhat obviously, because most of us couldn't afford to – but beyond financial motivation, never working would probably drive us insane. As humans, we need purpose – a reason to get up in the morning, and a focus for our day ahead. There's nothing wrong with Netflix, café lunches or mojitos, of course; but we need a balance.

There's much anecdotal evidence that work is good for our mental health, as it provides us with purpose and focus. We might slot into a sort of auto-pilot mode during the week; alarm, shower, dress, breakfast, teeth, commute, desk. And maybe the same in reverse at the end of the day. This gives us a routine. The bit in the middle might be more unpredictable, as work demands dictate the ebbs and flow. The start and end routine helps us prepare for the day ahead or decompress when we leave; all important functions to crank up and crank down.

Most of us would be pretty satisfied if we returned home from work and felt we had achieved something from the day. Maybe we have pushed forward on a task, completed a project, learnt something new, gained a fresh insight, enjoyed an exchange or discussion with a colleague or customer and so on. Often, we don't realize what we *do* achieve, and lump the totality of our work experience as 'work'; this means we lose out on the recognition of achievement and self-affirmation.

Rico

As a supervisor for the estates department at his local council, Rico was struggling with motivation in his job. He was capable, got on well with his team and met deadlines. In fact, he was doing exactly what the job required of him, and more. However, he had lost sight of *why* he was doing it. We explored a much wider picture of the consequences of his work and he was able to recollect scores of anecdotes from hugely appreciative council-house tenants. By widening his perspective, he rekindled his enthusiasm back to a level that made him love his job again.

Like Rico, we can all have slumps where we slot into the routine of work and fail to enjoy and appreciate the triumphs along the way. There may be an expectation for us to fulfil a series of triumphs… but that doesn't mean we shouldn't take stock, and bask in the occasional glory, where basking is due!

Work–life balance action
Listing achievements

As you close up at the end of each workday, list three achievements for the day – the best that you can find. Each needs to be something you made a conscious choice to achieve. It doesn't need to constitute a Nobel Peace Prize (though if you do achieve this, it should certainly go into your three achievements of the day!) – they are likely to be more piecemeal, such as 'finished the budget report' or 'received positive feedback from a client' or 'started a new recruitment project' or 'completed my appraisal' or even 'tidied my desk'. At the end of a five-day week you'll have 15 achievements. If this generates a warm, contented glow within you, then great. If it makes you recoil in disgust, it may be time to look for a new job.

An additional perspective to consider in this work–life balance action is the focus on our choices: we have chosen to actively engage with a task and progress it from point A to point B. When we feel stuck in a rut, or a lack of motivation, we often fail to recognize that we're actually making decisions, learning and achieving all the time.

If we're lucky, we may have transitioned into the work we're doing now because it grew from some embryonic interest and enthusiasm for the role. We might have got into social work because we had a desire to help people in difficult social situations or worked in engineering as we liked to construct things, or trained as a teacher because we enjoyed facilitating learning.

Not all of us are lucky though and may have found ourselves in back-breaking, mind-numbing and gut-wrenching jobs that we hate. Even in jobs we once liked, organizational change might have bulldozed in to make the role very different. I don't think I know anyone who has not, at some stage in their lives, taken on a job just for the pay cheque.

My first job in my early teens working on a potato production line at a farm was not taken out of my enjoyment of *batatas fritas* (that's Portuguese for French fries). I needed the money. Yet reflecting back to that role, I can see the embryonic emergence of my future career. What sustained me in the stinking, cold and repetitive role was enjoying the diverse people on the production line; they were all fascinating people in their own right. I've since carved a career based on my interest in people and how they tick.

What sparked your original passion for what you do? That first glimmer of interest must have come from somewhere. What interests us might take time to evolve and might not be immediately obvious. Whilst we all appreciate that there's no such thing as a job for life, the same might apply to careers. Many of us change careers along the way as we twist and turn, finding new meaning and purpose in what we do and the experiences we stumble across.

If a passion for what we do doesn't resonate, maybe this is saying we're not doing what's right for us. When I trained as a therapist in the mid-1990s, out of the 30 of us who completed the course, only three of us were active therapists four years later. The others found it suited them to do something different, albeit a variation on the therapist theme. However, this doesn't need to be fixed and final. I know a couple of graduates returned to being therapists many years later: it simply took them time to find their meaning and purpose.

Many people experience a split between what they believe they enjoy from work and the actual things that motivate them away from work. Some team-building exercises often begin with round-the-room introductions followed by the sharing of something other people might not know about you. I think these are brilliant as they share fascinating insights into experiences and achievements beyond what is known. I worked with a colleague for a year before such a team-building exercise offered me a new insight about him. Twice a year he would join battle re-enactment teams. He would dress up in the regalia of the particular historical re-enactment and join squads of fellow enthusiasts to scream and charge across the countryside. Brilliant!

I'm not sure such skills could be easily cross-transferable into his work but it demonstrates the diversity of experiences we might find if we have a look and give it a go. Maybe that was the point for this person; having a very different non-work interest so that his work persona was not the exclusive element of who he was.

As we see from work–life balance, it may help to connect our work and non-work lives so they become the whole of who we are, rather than disparate and disconnected separates which spar with each other. It might not be possible or feasible to find this synergy, but it has to be an opportunity to consider.

Work occupies a huge amount of our time, effort and lives. Creating a successful work–life balance is about modulating, modifying and moderating our life experiences. I've worked with many people over the years whose work persona has defined who they are. There's nothing wrong with this per se and it can help us forge a very enjoyable career. The point is about not losing, or forgetting about, ourselves in it.

Blair

I remember meeting Blair, a former chief financial officer for a global investment firm, who had garnered applause and praise wherever he went. He was brilliant at and in his job. But when he retired, he no longer had the same red-carpet treatment rolled out in front of him. It made him realize that the red carpet had been about 'what' he was, rather than 'who' he was as a person. The carpet came with the title of the job. He appreciated that the perks are often the things that keep you in a job and offer the glitz and glamour attributable to the role but they can come and go. Blair made the transition easily and found his work–life balance solution, quite possibly facilitated by a small vineyard he now tends in Tuscany.

Purpose and meaning are inextricably linked to how we see ourselves at work. Do we feed our purpose, or does it feed us? Do I act, feel and think like a therapist? Probably. Or is this some stereotype that I fall into? Society, culture, and the implicit and explicit norms of our organizations all shape together a set of behaviours and traits associated with how we perform or are in our work. Maybe we do what we do because our way of being is conducive to the role we adopt? These philosophical questions are fascinating – but a practical question is whether this tension works *for* us, or generates some sense of conflict.

Creating a successful work–life balance involves ensuring we fit within our work world. Whether we adapt to our job or the job adapts to us, we need to feel at one with why we do what we do. If we don't, then we're likely to generate feelings of stress or tension as we struggle to fit our round pin in a square hole.

Something which considerably helps us enjoy our work, above and beyond the role we inhabit, is the fact that we get paid for it. We all need to make a living and to earn an income. Ask a 10-year-old what they want to do when they grow up and many today will say they want to be 'rich and famous'. As we get a bit more mature, we realize it's not quite as easy as that, nor, perhaps, what we really need. Purpose and meaning kicks into gear.

Aspiration and mission

Some of the students I see at my university have chosen subjects like law and medicine because they know if they do well they will earn a good wage. But in my experience, this is not the student body's main driver – instead, the vast majority study these subjects because they believe in what they do. For some, money's a bonus but not the be-all and end-all.

There's no simple elixir to finding purpose. It has a very individual meaning and construct. What gives me purpose might be very different to you. The key is being open to a range of experiences; some will resonate, some won't. Battle re-enactments don't really do it for me but have you thought about what it might offer you: team-work, competitiveness, grounding-in-history, fresh-air, exercise, screaming?

In a work context, purpose allows us to develop skills and challenge ourselves sufficiently. Ultimately, we need to enjoy what we do but where do we start? We can be influenced by parents, family and friends. This might be an opportunity to construct your purpose dream team, whereby you identify 10 contacts in different types of jobs; speak to them, understand what drives them or shadow them at their work.

When I knew that farming and, in particular, the potato production line, was not the career for me, my parents set me up with a family friend who worked as a stockbroker in a city firm. I got a week's work experience which was fascinating but, ultimately, not for me.

Finding purpose is as much finding out what connects with us as it is about what does not. We need the opportunity to experience, in order to open up a pathway of intrigue and interest. We may benefit from parental guidance, direction and encouragement, but it has to be at the right pace. If we feel railroaded into a particular work trajectory we might react adversely to this. Conversely, limited encouragement might breed apathy and demotivation. We need to find what fits who we are and what gives us satisfaction, enjoyment and challenge.

Psychological contract

Whether we are forging a new career path or bedding down our current one, our relationship with our job, or rather our organization, is an important one. We might gain remuneration and a sense of work identity but there's more to it than work. The psychological contract is a term used to describe the more informal expectations between us, as employee, and our organization, as employer.

We are usually interviewed for a job on the basis that we meet essential and desirable criteria for a job description. On the basis we conform to this and get offered the job, the contract of employment sets out the core conditions for our role – the work expected and the 'benefits' in return. The psychological contract goes beyond this, to include elements of our work which create more meaning and value. Whilst salary is important, perhaps training, advancement and development might emerge as more beneficial.

Beyond the formal contract of employment, we might elicit evolving expectations which, although not written down, give us a boost of encouragement and motivation. A classic case is when we sniff an opportunity to gain advancement or promotion if we fulfil certain, and usually unspecified, criteria. The problem is this can be a gamble which may not pay off.

The contract of employment has our terms of work clear and unambiguous. The psychological contract, however, is largely unclear and ambiguous. Both are as important as each other. The former is more functional and practical, giving us a route map for what is demanded of us – the *what* we do. The psychological contract, however, exists largely through the inter-relationships and unspoken, implicit rules of engagement – the *how* we do it.

Organizations are weighed down by disgruntled employees who have had hopes dashed based on a misguided set of expectations, or psychological contract. If we put in more than we feel we get in return, then the psychological contract has effectively been breached. When this happens, the relationship between us and our workplace can break down, sometimes terminally. The impact on work–life balance splinters accordingly, and we're likely to grumble away doing the bare minimum or leave.

Being politically astute

Being 'politically astute' is not about trying to understand government policy; rather, it's politics with a small 'p' – the micro-politics of everyday life, the day-to-day decisions and choices which influence our personal and professional identity, relationships and aspirations. Developing an intuition radar for these unspoken, unwritten signals of organizational life (including the various forms of communication and listening that were discussed in Chapter 2 is one way that we can limit the potential of a breached psychological contract.

There's no cast-iron rule book here; rather it's about learning how people are and how they behave. It might come as a bit of a shock but sometimes people don't tell the truth. Even when they do, it might be a partial truth or an embellishment of the truth.

Veronika

After two years working towards a partnership at her architectural corporation, Veronika found the position had gone to a colleague. As we talked through her intense disappointment and confusion, we started to unpick what had happened. It transpired that there had been miscommunication and misunderstanding between Veronika and her boss about what steps she would need to take to improve her prospects for partnership. The ambiguity and misread signals heightened Veronika's hopefulness, and misdirected the efforts she was making to progress.

We can best seek out the implicit politics of our environment by listening and watching. What's going on around us? What are people talking about formally, and importantly, what's also happening below the surface? What are the fears and hopes, anxieties and enthusiasms? What's the pulse of the department? Doing this can help us develop a social radar or group empathy which resonates with our intuition and 'gut feeling'.

Body language and facial cues can tell us more than words. Our boss might be buttering us up with the lure of a promotion based on our next big project but if they're saying this with crossed arms, looking down at the ground or shiftily scratching their nose, we're likely to pick up something contradictory here. The signs might not be quite so obvious as this, of course, but even the absence of normally fixed eye-contact can signal more than – well, than meets the eye.

It's not all about how other people behave, though. Knowing when to be tactful, diplomatic or assertive can influence how others react to us and how we get things done. If we spot signs of mistrust in others, we have the opportunity to become more transparent, open, congruent and honest with others to model how we like to be. Maybe we need to demonstrate confidence and assuredness in some contexts but reflectiveness and pensiveness in others.

Each organization, department and team is different because they're made up of a diverse community of unique individuals with their own blend of hopes and dreams, motivators and drivers. The attitude, approach and commitment to work can also influence the dynamics. The secret is about building up this unwritten awareness of what's going on below the surface. This takes time and can't readily be built up as soon as we jump into a new role.

Getting on in our work requires us to manage this unspoken, implicit world. It will help us communicate what's important to us and better understand expectations of us from our organizations. Through this, we can find improved ways to enjoy and connect with our work and in so doing better juggle the ingredients of our work–life balance.

Mentoring and guidance

Mentoring is a resource offered by many organizations, where a mentor is usually an experienced member of staff assigned to a newer or less experienced mentee. Part of a mentor's role is to offer guidance and insight in navigating the unique organizational pathway as well as understanding how to help develop the mentee up and through the organization.

Though we may not always need a mentor to navigate this path, it can certainly help. The principle remains the same: understanding who might be the 'movers and shakers', the people with influence and responsibility, because it's not always clear.

In one of my first jobs at the age of 20, I spent time getting to know a particular director and partner of an organization I wanted to work for. This included my funding a few trips to Starbucks, but it paid off and bingo, I got the job I wanted. I continued to nurture this relationship, learnt a huge amount from him and saw myself emulating his pathway. However, one day he announced to the company he was leaving for a lucrative new job opportunity. Within a week, my organizational guardian angel flew away and this mentoring torch was snuffed out. I'd spent so long focusing on this one person that I'd failed to nurture, grow and develop other relationships. This required me to change course and find ways to connect with others.

The lesson here perhaps is to spread the bets and consider a selection of horses, so to speak. We can't rely on one person, or anyone really, to shepherd us up the organizational ladder or along the tightrope.

This is a big part of work–life balance because a huge amount of time can be gained or lost by how we tread through this labyrinth. As we discussed in Chapter 2, our dream team can be a very influential group of people who can help contribute to our advancement and development, as well as day-to-day support when we need it. It also links into how we network and nurture the relationships we choose to develop.

Work–life balance action
Impact of people at work

Have a think about people in your working environment and how they impact on your work life:

- Who makes the key decisions or holds the budgets?
- Who do you trust most and why?
- Who do you trust least and why?
- Who is most influential in your career development?
- Who is likely to be your greatest threat to your career development?
- Who is reliable, conscientious and productive?
- Who gossips the most?
- Who do you need to be wary or careful of and why?
- Who can you speak to when you're in a crisis or stressed?

Trust is so important in life at work, and yet there's no rule book or training programme. The person who smiles at you sweetly every day in passing might be the person who sticks the metaphorical boot in when you least expect it. Of course, that's not to say we need to go around suspicious of everyone – that would be no way to live, in my opinion – but trust does need to be earned. And this goes both ways, remember; how will you demonstrate that you can be trusted? Wisdom and experience come from knowing who to trust, why we trust them, how we trust them and when. Ultimately, the people we identify as our trusted colleagues will be the people we can rely on, and who will help us best manage our work–life balance.

Professional development

Swimming through the murky, uncharted sea of organizational life is not all about finding ways to climb the corporate ladder. As processes change, technology advances and companies adapt to stay ahead of the competition, we may need to develop ourselves just to keep up. We might know the pecking order of our team and where we 'fit', but people come and go, and new recruits may emerge with more experience or better skills than us.

If we have the skills to do our job, we're going to do it better and faster than if we don't which, of course, feeds into our choices surrounding work–life balance. Some of our developmental needs might be clear, but with others, we may need to take time to plan for long-term goals. The first step is assessing if we have enough for now. Then it's about anticipating future needs, demands and trends.

A 'counsellor' in the UK is currently not a protected title, meaning anyone can call themselves a counsellor. Our professional body, the British Association for Counselling and Psychotherapy (there are equally reputable alternatives) does require registered members to meet minimum criteria for membership. For many counsellors, this has been sufficient to get work. BACP also offers accreditation for those who meet a higher set of criteria; a lengthy and arduous process. In the past, the majority of counsellors chose not to become accredited because there were plenty of jobs that did not require this. As more people are attracted to counselling as a career, supply now outstrips demand, meaning recruiters are increasingly asking for accredited counsellors. Economics has set the bar higher.

Goalposts can and do move. In my field of counselling, supply and demand have determined the need for increased professional development. Conversely, the 'oil and gas capital of Europe', Aberdeen, has suffered a dramatic economic slump over the last five years. In 2012, a barrel of crude oil hit nearly $130, then plummeted in 2016 to about $25. In the north-east of Scotland, everyone was affected by the tsunami of redundancies. And yet now, in mid-2019, the price has drifted up to about $75, making the industry profitable again. Those who were made redundant largely left the sector, meaning that now the sector is screaming out for recruits, offering juicy incentives reminiscent of the oil-rush years.

All of this is to say that whilst we might think we have the skills for today based largely on time served, sometimes we need that little bit of paper that gives us the qualification, award or certificate – never mind the additional learning that goes in to *gaining* that little bit of paper.

As we consider what we should strive for in our professional development, it is worth pondering on whether we need to improve on the things we are not good at or focus on the things where our strengths lie – in balancing your efforts across your work and the rest of your life, where can your energy and investment have the most impact?

Tip

Even with a qualification, we may find that some awarding bodies are regarded in higher esteem than others. It is well worth the investment of time, effort and energy to scope out the more reputable and recognized qualification-awarding professional associations, and to consider a cost–benefit calculation on the merits of professional development.

Mitch

Mitch was a successful landscape gardener with a small team of freelance 'helpers'. He came to see me because he'd kept hearing that he needed to engage in social media, to 'build up his profile' – except he hated computers, and hated social media even more. He wanted me to instil some magical enthusiasm into him to do what he was resisting. However, when we audited his business and assessed his own skillset, we concluded that his current strategy was actually bang on, and it was dubious whether his time on social media would pay back sufficiently. It turned out that Mitch had a great rapport with his customers, and it was this which maintained a steady flow of work, and generated more opportunities through word of mouth.

Even better – through taking on this evaluation, we also discovered he was a bit lax in his accounts management, which meant some customers didn't pay him on time or at all, and his team got frustrated from fluctuating and sporadic wages. His solution was to bring in a new accounts software package (a simple one) and spend more routine time on this, instead of on the dreaded 'online presence'. As a result, he improved his cashflow, allowing him to pay a more-than-willing helper to run his social media, in a way in which he could only have dreamt of.

As we consider how to develop ourselves professionally, an interesting reverse perspective often pays dividends. Spending time helping others to develop not only helps them and the team, but it can reinforce and consolidate our own skills. Then, the people we help often find a way to help us in return. Win–win!

Work–life balance action
SWOT analysis

You might be familiar with the SWOT analysis model, but it's worth applying it to your professional development needs and revising and refreshing it regularly. The SWOT analysis is credited to

Albert Humphrey from Stamford University in the 1960s (though he denies it, so the origin is unclear). Whoever came up with it, though, is an unsung hero.

The examples below may or may not resonate with you, so adapt them to fit you and your work world. Strengths and weaknesses are normally more internal to you or personal, whereas opportunities and threats are largely external. The one consistent topic applicable to each category is 'people-relationships', and where they help or hinder:

STRENGTHS	experiences, training, achievements, values, work-ethic, integrity, flexibility
WEAKNESSESS	limitations, skills deficiencies, stress management, delegation skills, procrastination
OPPORTUNITIES	mentoring, networking, connections, reputation and professional profile
THREATS	external and internal competition and change, new systems and processes, including IT

Whilst this model applies to the working life, it is necessary to cast some thought over the impact on our non-work life. A new qualification could open new professional opportunities, but if it requires longer working days, how would this fit with our work–life balance? Whilst we might not have work–life balance on our mind all the time, we should be thinking of what decisions are influencing it.

Quest for knowledge

There's only so much we can possibly know. We may know what we know… but do we know what we *don't* know? Who knows! Education systems can put emphasis on the acquisition of knowledge sometimes, arguably at the expense of learning about thoughts, feelings, emotions, how to act, how to be and how to live our lives.

I remember learning that King Harold II of England was killed by an arrow in his eye at the Battle of Hastings in 1066, but I'm not quite sure how knowing this has improved my life. I do feel sorry for Harold though. It must have been really painful.

Our education allows us to pass through a series of academic benchmarks which help us at each stage to step up the ladder, from primary or junior school to high or senior school, then maybe college or university, possibly postgraduate training and so on. Whatever stage of life we're in, the pursuit of these qualifications can be stressful. We do what we can, and hope that we achieve the grades or results we seek. Each set of results opens a new and different pathway ahead. There's pressure on us to perform and deliver: from parents, family, friends and from peers, but probably most comes from our own high expectations of ourselves.

So how do we manage this ongoing step-by-step pressure? In my experience, a dose of reality can give us a stress inoculation. We're not all going to be the brainy top-of-the-class whizz-kid – and outside of the stressful environment of exams or tests, being the top of the class isn't what will matter the most to all of us. What matters more, to more people in more situations, is to develop a curious and inquisitive disposition – so we find the way to enjoy *learning* and finding out about things, as opposed to the rote acquisition of knowledge.

Here are a couple of examples of what I mean. I can think of a couple of PhD students at my university who, during their course of counselling, reflected on what got them to where they were today. Ali, a botanist, could track back to her fascination with insects, which began when she was about five years old and she saved a drowsy bee; and Stefan, an engineer, could remember taking old radio sets to bits, despite the fact he could never seem to put them back together again.

We learn by testing and exploring, even though we may not always know where we are going. It's the journey of discovery that sets in motion our innate curiosity. A key part of learning is making mistakes. Not necessarily on purpose, of course – but Stefan might have forged his career path precisely because he wanted to learn how to put things back together again.

Mistakes are not necessarily 'bad' or wrong, and neither should they be avoided. Otherwise we'll never learn. Sometimes we need to take risks to understand and appreciate our boundaries and limitations. Danny MacAskill, a world-renowned Scottish stunt cyclist, has amassed a collection of online videos demonstrating his awe-inspiring acrobatics. He has also amassed quite a number of broken bones over the years and yet this simply propels him, in all senses, to refine and perfect his skills. He is continually learning, pushing his boundaries and achieving ever more feats of skill and endurance.

From a health, safety and common-sense perspective, whilst mistakes can represent a valuable learning experience, we need to understand the potential consequences. Risk management is a crucial part of the learning. Danny's talent undoubtedly includes his assessment of the risk matched against the bike's capabilities and his acute performance skills.

If we think back to our childhood, some of the most memorable experiences will have included situations which had an unexpected outcome. Not knowing or not expecting allows us to absorb the richness of experiences and bear the fruits of newness. If life was predictable, it would be pretty boring. The unknown is not just crucial but a necessity.

We're not always going to know things on our own. Other people might have the answers and it becomes about knowing who to ask and when. We shouldn't feel embarrassed to ask questions, or to share our knowledge if someone asks. We tend to like it when someone asks us a question which we can answer; it feeds our own quest for learning.

I used to work with a colleague who had been a finalist on the BBC knowledge quiz, *Mastermind*. He had a brain the size of a planet. He just seemed to know everything. He was a voracious reader and simply enjoyed learning and testing his knowledge. The M8 is a 60-mile-long motorway joining Edinburgh and Glasgow and, like all such roads in the UK, has distance markers every 100 metres to pinpoint locations in the event of accidents. He had memorized the numbers for each marker location and could tell you where you were at any point of the motorway. Genius. Why did he need to know this? He didn't – but commuting that stretch piqued his interest.

For us mere mortals who might struggle to remember a conversation we had even yesterday, our brains may require us to focus on knowing what we need to know. It's also about accepting the limits to our knowledge and being OK with that, rather than ramping up the stress stakes and panicking about knowledge gaps.

We might mindlessly consume content on our phones when we're at a loose end, checking the news, searching Gumtree or flicking through Instagram… and that's fine, good even – but why not have a go learning something new? Find out the source of a phrase you use, look for a different recipe for a favourite dish, learn a new word for the day, seek out information about a bird or plant you noticed recently, explore how something works, etc. The options are pretty much infinite, and I'd suggest much more satisfying than looking at a friend's holiday snaps from Benidorm!

Most successful entrepreneurs are not actually superhuman. What they often have in common is accepting their own limits and having the gumption to bring in advice, skills, knowledge and expertise from those who can plug the gaps. This is what also makes a team function optimally; having a diversity of talent so that the synergy effect provides the totality of capability.

It can be a relief to know that we don't need to know everything, whilst appreciating that we can gain huge emotional, psychological and intellectual nourishment by choosing to be open to learning. Letting the roots of our creativity grow, allows us to craft our unique arbour of branches.

Elva

In her final year of her PhD reading philosophy and politics, Elva came to see me with acute anxiety associated with her pending thesis submission. This was the culmination of nine years of academic study entering its final furlong, from undergraduate degree, Master's and beyond. Was the thesis good enough? We broke it down into a) was it good enough for her and b) was it good enough to gain her PhD? In order, No and Yes. For her, she could spend the rest of her life learning more about her unique topic, yet it was entirely sufficient to achieve her PhD. Job done. Pat on the back. Elva's quest for knowledge was met and satisfied by ending this particular chapter, before needing to move to the next stage in her career.

Creating a successful work–life balance involves the pursuit of knowledge in all forms, whether it involves parenting, understanding personal finances or becoming an expert in our field of work. There's no real end-point in mind, just keeping up the inclination, enthusiasm, joy and passion for learning.

Adapting to a new role or job

We all experience being 'the new kid on the block' at various stages in our lives, whether this is in an organization, starting self-employment, moving home or after a significant life event. It can take a lot of time and effort to know what we need to do and how. Showing enthusiasm and proving our worth is important, but we also need to pace ourselves and appreciate that it will take time to acquire knowledge and skills. Taking on too many tasks can lead to burnout, which can be counter-productive to making a positive impression.

If we're starting a new job, the job description given at the application stage can give some guidance for what might be expected of us, and inductions may exist to give us some organizational context. Understanding the essentials of the work, however, will come with experience and with doing the job every day.

We all have different needs when we start out. For some, we'll just want to be left to get on with it, whilst others may need a more structured, guided pathway. Understanding and communicating our needs will facilitate the transition over the initial days and offer some structure. Even with the best structure in the world, though, a new role can be stressful precisely *because* it's new, and we're learning to understand the dynamics of the work environment as well as our specific role within it.

We're also building new relationships. Some of our colleagues may welcome us with open arms and a genuine, enthusiastic smile. Others might be more cautious and wary, unsure of who we are, how we tick and what our motives might be. Trust needs to be built on all sides from ground zero.

It helps to consider the undercurrents and background context. It's rare for a workplace context not to have some sort of emotional baggage; maybe there have been team disagreements in the past which still linger, or some residual fallout from recent redundancy threats, or a general feeling of uneasiness due to organizational change. All of this can create a toxicity which we can get drawn into, unwittingly and unwillingly. It's about knowing where and how to stand our ground and choose carefully how we add our presence to a complex situation. If we agree, empathize or sympathize, this could be interpreted as collusion – but if we shun the topic, we might be seen as being distant or not a team player. It's a tricky balance, and time will tell if our response or reaction is the correct one for us.

The work–life balance component of adapting to a new role or job is potentially massive. How much time and effort can we put in or do we need to put in? Some situations may require us to jump in with both feet, put in more time that we might want. However, if our team or bosses spot the huge effort we're making, might this evolve into an expectation for the future? How do we find the balance when everything's new?

We will fit somewhere on the organizational hierarchy and our attitude and behaviour will influence our way of being at work. This is for us to determine how to pitch this work persona as it's going to be how people view or evaluate us. We might find being the team joker endears us to our colleagues but could conflict with others' view of our professionalism. Conversely, if we're too serious and avoid joining in, we might be regarded as aloof. We all want to work with people who make our work lives more enjoyable; sometimes this is having a sense of humour, sometimes it's not. We have to work out what's appropriate in a sort of social empathic awareness.

Reviews and feedback are helpful measures of performance, so regular 'check-ins' can be invaluable. Keep-In-Touch meetings (KITs) offer an opportunity to discuss both formal work issues and more generalized informal aspects to a role. If you're a manager, try them with your team. If you have a manager or boss, ask for one with them. This is all positive professional development material.

Most new jobs will come with a probationary period, within which we need to demonstrate that we're actually doing the job we're employed to do. It gives employers a contractual window when our employment can be rescinded or ended if we do not meet the grade. It also gives us a chance to consider if the job is right for us or not. Clearly, this is a crucial time period, which sets in motion how we adapt to our role. Some organizations are more pernickety about this than others, so gauging expectations is critical. We might have slaved over a job application form, blushed our way through the interview and landed our plum job: but it doesn't end there. This is only the beginning.

Simone

After a career in management, Simone jumped into small business wholesaling fancy goods for the local retail market. She had accurately spotted a niche and quickly built up a successful supply chain, which required her to recruit support staff. On paper, her team of five were well suited and had good administrative and operational experience for the role. But none of them stayed long, all quickly leaving the business. Simone increasingly found her greatest angst was recruiting and retaining staff. We conducted an anonymous written exit interview for her departing employees, and soon found out some interesting trends. Simone had a habit of both making unreasonable workload demands, and coming across as very much superior and aloof, which caused people to feel demeaned, unappreciated and disrespected. Whilst unnerving for Simone to receive this feedback, it allowed her to address 'her issues' and improve her relationship with her staff.

Table 3.1 Self-assessment

	Outstanding	Meets expectations	Needs improvement	Unsatisfactory	Change strategy?
Communication					
Feedback					
Delegation					
Productivity					
Attendance					
Professionalism					
Team-work					
Resourceful					
Decision-making					
Creative					
Dependable					
Flexible					
Leadership					
Engagement					

Supportive				
Work quality				
Initiative				
Integrity				
Knowledge				
Personable				

As Simone found, relationships are key in establishing yourself in a new role or job, whether you're the boss or one of the team. Many employee appraisals and reviews now tend to invite appraisees to provide upward feedback about their boss. The 360-degree feedback is also used for similar purposes. It doesn't need us to wait for formal processes. We can simply ask, 'how am I doing?'.

Work–life balance action
Self-assessment

It's worth keeping an eye on professional performance by rating yourself, or getting others to feed back to you. This may give you some advance warning to adapt further or change.

Go through the list in Table 3.1 (or compile your own list), rating yourself from 'unsatisfactory' to 'outstanding'. If you have the chance, you could also ask some trusted people who know your work to rate you as well; but make sure you can trust them not to give you falsely positive ratings!

When you have identified your areas of strength and your areas for development, use the right-hand column to jot down some notes on ideas for how you can make necessary changes. The aim is to maintain or enhance what you're doing well already, or to make adjustments to areas you need to improve.

Managing change

Change is the one constant in our lives, especially at work. How we cope with change at work invariably impacts on our work–life balance. We need to keep up with trends, develop new, better and improved ways of doing things, respond and adapt to customer behaviour and keep one step ahead of the competition, whether this is organizational or amongst colleagues.

Managing change that happens to you

Despite the unchanging-ness of change, most of us don't like it. We prefer what's safe and familiar, and to understand the framework in which we operate. When there's some threat to the status quo, we often retrench and retaliate against the unfamiliar and the unwelcome. This resistance occurs because the experience of change can feel like a loss of the known and a shift into new territory. Perhaps – as with any loss – we need to reflect on what has gone before, so we can mark and process it and move on. Fear of change can be more impactful than the change itself, especially if we catastrophize and blow out of proportion the consequences and fallout. When we look back on change, it is rarely as bad as we feared; often, we'll see how it makes sense and has been positive. But we wouldn't want to admit that, would we?

Admittedly, some change is far from positive, at least not at the time. For example, when major employers in an area close or relocate, this can be utterly devastating to the local community in various ways, beyond the immediate loss of employment. It can take decades for the locality to recover, if it does at all. It might never be the same again, or as it was; but that doesn't mean we should lose hope. In many situations, communities will adapt to the changes with new community groups, social enterprises and working collectives that didn't exist before.

In the late 1990s, I was contracted by a global multinational corporation to support a team of 20 high-earning sales staff who were to learn whether they had kept their jobs or would be offered a severance package. I was allocated a couple of hours with each of them over the course of a week to help them adjust to, and cope with, their change.

Seven of the 20 kept their jobs; the others were given quite a generous severance package. With my empathic demeanour at the ready and prepared for a spectrum of intense and volatile emotions, I was unexpectedly confronted by unanimous glee and excitement. It appeared that everyone had evaluated the pros and cons of both options and accepted either that came their way.

This made me realize that change can be better accommodated if we know more about the context and rationale because we can then evaluate the consequences and opportunities sufficiently. This can also be achieved by acknowledging the emotions associated with the change and feelings of any losses which may or may not emerge. Getting facts helps to take away ambiguity and uncertainty which can be the drivers of emotional overload.

Conor

After working up from an internship to the position of salaried copywriter at a public relations agency, Conor was in charge of the creative output for a large utilities company. He was good at his job and had won several awards for his work. When the contract went out to tender, his agency lost out. Though he had had very little influence over the negotiation of the contract, Conor was unceremoniously 'sacked' because the contract was not available any more to pay for his wages. Conor felt that it was unfair, unjust and unnecessary and it took him a considerable time to regain his confidence. After processing his loss, he wanted to have greater control over his work, and decided to become a freelance copywriter. His skills did the talking and won him significant pieces of work.

Managing change within your remit

It's one thing to be a victim of change which has been imposed on us, but it's another to be an architect of it. In many stages in life, we'll be the person who needs to make changes: these may be personal decisions in order to recalibrate our work–life balance, or changes for the benefit of teams we're part of. Most change doesn't happen just for the sake of it: as the popular saying goes, if it ain't broken, it doesn't need fixing.

The more consideration and effort that goes into crafting a damage-limiting change strategy, the more chance there will be of it being effective. If we appreciate some resistance as a bottom line, we can prepare to offset anxieties early on and understand the background context. Timing factors into this: we need to give the right amount of time to work through the process, but not so much that it becomes counter-productive.

Here's an example. I was brought in, late in the process, to a call centre that had announced they were moving to a new purpose-built location. On the face of it, the building was a significant improvement in terms of space and facilities. It was only one mile away from the previous location. However, staff had not been consulted or sufficiently primed. This led to much anxiety and anger. The tension was largely associated with this lack of communication and how the employees felt secondary to the functional move. It was also going to impact those who had crafted schooling and homecare arrangements for the previous location. Whilst many adjusted to the change, the goodwill damage had been done.

Whilst this example involved a relatively short distance change, sometimes organizations make much more significant decisions, making it impossible for some employees to reconcile or manage. This can trigger a potentially huge upheaval, especially for those with families. Sometimes, a work–life balance means making a tough decision to leave a difficult and unsustainable working situation: staying in an uncomfortable environment can have adverse effects on our physical and mental wellbeing, our relationships at home and our focus at work. It's important to consider all these aspects of the situation, because though there will be income-related consequences, health might be a greater priority.

Change needs to be *decisive*, not *divisive*. This is achieved through the factual clarity of why the change is happening and, importantly, how. The 'how' bit tends to open up the consequences and opportunities. It might be a bit of a mindset shift too. We can resist change but this usually creates an external and internal conflict in itself. We might struggle with a huge amount of emotional angst, frustration and tension but what purpose does this serve? It may mean we'll take home this stress and infect our domestic work–life balance.

Options for what we can do will differ depending on our situation but is likely to include acknowledging and managing our emotional response, guarding against negative or catastrophizing thinking, and possibly changing our behaviour. The behaviour bit may involve asking questions about the change, collaborating with others or setting in place how we can acquire any new resources, tools or skills to absorb the change.

Alternatively, we need to somehow adapt and integrate the changes into a new way forward. Will the change make improvements in our work lives? Might it offer new opportunities we did not have before? Can we find a way that this might actually improve our work–life balance? Adapting to change usually involves the capacity to communicate, collaborate and participate.

We all want to sail through change and become champions of it but resistance, to some degree, is normal. It's our responsibility how we choose to respond. We might think we don't have any choice in relation to the change, and that might be true to some degree, but we can choose how we feel, think and act in relation to it. Work–life balance is about making choices about where and how we channel ourselves within our work environment. It's a learning process and no one's perfect.

Reality of perfectionism

Many of us strive for perfectionism; but there's a big difference between doing something perfectly and doing something to the best of our abilities. Perfectionism is often forged in earlier life if we felt valued only by our accomplishments. This leads us to seek out and yearn for approval or external validation. In this way, our self-worth is defined by what we achieve, not by who we are. If we only derived approval from our successes then this can expose us to a sensitivity to our self-esteem. The perception of needing to be perfect can be our defence against criticism and judgement.

In pretty much all scenarios, we fail to reach that high expectation which, in turn, drives us to perform even better the next time, which feeds the vicious cycle further. We never reach that unassail-able peak yet this doesn't stop us exhausting ourselves trying. It just feeds the expectation monster and creates further guilt, self-blame and self-loathing.

Maintaining work–life balance involves having *achievable* ex-pectations of ourselves. Spending an inordinate amount of time and effort on unrealistic goals can generate angst and frustration, and means losing precious space that could be focused on more pleasurable and rewarding experiences.

Steve

After a succession of short-term relationships, Steve wanted to consider if this was just hard luck and bad choices (for him) or whether he was, in some way, colluding with the problem. His partners just didn't 'tick all the boxes', as he put it. It emerged that academically, as an expert in his field of applied mathematics, he had this capacity to always solve complex problems. He was, in a way, used to perfection. This solution focus peppered his non-work life and he had developed an expectation that he could solve relationship challenges similarly. He ended the relationships because they failed to meet his absolute perfection. In time, he was able to split the focus, so he could realistically maintain his solution focus at work whilst adopting a more accepting and real perspective in relationships.

Steve was able to understand his relationship predicament pre-cisely because his PhD had given such limited learning opportunity. He began to value some wriggle-room in how relationships ebb and flow. It reflects the issue of perfectionism we all experience: our determination to be perfect means we're probably not appreciating the quest to improve. Despite what we might think sometimes, life would be a bit boring if we didn't have opportunities to learn and we would have a lesser understanding of achievement.

In the mid-1990s I decided to take my motorbike test, and after a couple of intensive training weekends found myself nervously biking up to the local test centre, my visor steaming up from hyperventilation. Thankfully (perhaps more for other road users!), there was limited traffic around the test circuit, and when the exam was complete, I was somewhat shocked to find I received a 'perfect score' from the instructor. A wee bit of me was quite pleased... but a much bigger part of me was aware I was still a novice with a huge amount to learn. The perfect score hadn't identified areas I needed to improve through experience.

Work–life balance involves enjoying aspects of learning and development as part of our drive for meaning and purpose, as discussed in Chapter 1. The opportunity to learn creates a crucial motivating factor in itself.

An additional issue in the myth of the perfectionism bubble is how we often compare and rate ourselves against other people. It's quite normal to identify differences between ourselves and perhaps use this as a driver for us to emulate their skills or competencies, if that's what the comparison is about. However, if the quest is overly strong we may risk losing part of who we are and our personal identity. The antidote here is to enjoy, appreciate and celebrate who we are, accepting differences.

Making mistakes

As I mentioned earlier in this chapter, it's important to give ourselves permission to take risks and make mistakes, especially when we're developing an acceptance strategy for perfectionism. We're often preoccupied with a fear of making mistakes in the belief that we'll look stupid or inept. However, if we don't make mistakes and take risks, we'll lose the opportunity to learn from them.

Making mistakes can inform a future framework for decision-making, enabling us to make choices about our actions through this learnt experience. Being perfect doesn't give us this resilience or a capacity to actively think about risk management. This resonates with a wider aspect of work–life balance as learning about decision-making and choices crosses over home and work. We can just as easily become overloaded with demands on us at home and work. How we respond to these can help to limit or mitigate potential stress responses.

Face the fear

Perfectionism is often reinforced by a sense of fear, associated with being seen to be imperfect. Sometimes it can help to consider what this fear factor is about and how real it is. What is it that we fear and how real is it? Are we catastrophizing? Are we in the real world here? Importantly, does it really matter in the grand scheme of things? So what if we make the odd slip-up? It might cause a temporary embarrassment, if at all; but this will be short-lived, and the lessons learnt might be invaluable. In this way, a cost–benefit analysis can help us develop a more realistic perspective. Might the benefit of the learning outweigh the cost of that anxiety?

Samuel

Confident in most aspects of his job, public speaking was an intense fear for Samuel. His anxiety was associated with being in front of a roomful of people staring at him and – in his mind – judging him. This put pressure on him to be perfect... yet it was this perfectionism that caused the fear. There was too much that could go wrong: problems with the audiovisual equipment, he might lose his train of thought, he might say the wrong thing or stop in mid-flow. He could never be *perfect*. When we practised public speaking in our session, we made it a fun experience, and he learnt to not just accept but even laugh at some of his inadvertent slip-ups. They were genuinely funny. I wasn't judging him, so this fear factor slowly disappeared. He became more confident by speaking to progressively larger groups of people, from family and friends to trusted work colleagues and this built up to the large group he originally feared most. He didn't need to be perfect. He needed to be real.

'Get a Life' needs audit scaling system: professional issues

The scaling system in the table below applies for each section discussed in this chapter and is based on your personal perception of whether there is a deficiency, imbalance or need… or not. Everyone is different so there's no right or wrong. This simply allows you to consider the gaps that exist for you.

The scoring uses a self-rating percentage index from 0–100 with 0 per cent referring to needs totally **unmet** and 100 per cent equating to needs totally **met**. Add up the percentage totals and divide this by the number of sections to give you a total percentage for this chapter. At the end of the book, you will have a percentage total for each chapter, giving you scope to consider where you need to prioritize action.

If any sections are irrelevant to you, ignore them and reduce the number of sections you divide this by accordingly.

	Sections	Percentage of needs currently met %
1	Purpose and meaning at work	
2	Politically astute	
3	Mentoring and guidance	
4	Professional development	
5	Quest for knowledge and learning	
6	Managing a new role or job	
7	Coping with change	
8	Perfectionism	
Total Score for Chapter 3 (out of 800%): Professional issues		
Divide this Total Score by **8**		
Total Percentage Score (out of 100%) for Chapter 3		

Figure 3.1   Professional issues needs audit radar

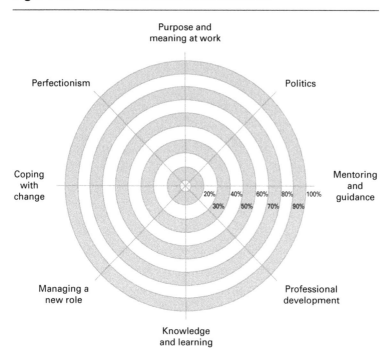

For the more visually minded, plot a dot on the radar diagram (Figure 3.1) with the same percentage scale: 0 for needs totally unmet up to 100 per cent for needs totally met. You can then join the dots together to form a needs audit radar. This method gives you a visual cue to identify the gaps in your needs.

This chapter on Professional Issues has focused on the wider aspect of why we work and some of key variables that shape our experience of life at work and where we sit within it. This provides a backdrop to motivation, professional development and competency in being at work. With a clearer perspective on these areas, we are better informed as to how we embrace our work lives, so we can better fit this into our work–life balance jigsaw picture.

The next chapter delves more deeply into Productivity and Performance, where I focus more on the essentials of what makes us effective in our work and how this impacts our work–life balance.

04
Productivity and performance

At the heart of creating a successful work–life balance is the need or ambition to work faster and smarter, so that we can accomplish more in the limited time we have. It's about quality, not quantity! So much of our time is wasted or poorly used. It's not necessarily our fault: it may be that we haven't had the time (perhaps ironically) or training to consider and plan how to be more productive in what we do. This chapter presents some ways we can improve our performance to aid our work–life balance.

Time management

Most of us don't actively or conscientiously manage our time; rather, we react to the demands that sail across our bows. As soon as the phone rings or the e-mail pings, we jump. Is this the most effective response for us? Maybe we need to change how we respond to distractions; to prioritize depending on the communication devices we have and how we use them at home or work.

I propel myself through the air like an Olympic netball player when our landline phone rings because only our close family use this for rare urgent issues. (Even *I* don't know my home landline number!) On the other hand, the greatest contribution to my work–life balance was undoubtedly finding a way to silence my mobile phone e-mail alerts, which in the past had been dinging away like an urgent Morse Code message.

Someone is phoning or e-mailing us because it suits them, but that doesn't mean it's convenient or necessary for us to respond immediately. The confusion emerges when **we** want a fast response from someone, so we make contact in the hope or assumption that **they** will be immediately available. This expectation builds on us a comparative need to respond similarly. Modern-day technologies have also advanced so much that, with the numerous ways we have to communicate, there are further expectations of immediacy (I sometimes reflect with fondness on the days before mobile phones and the internet). The reality is, we don't always need to respond immediately to messages and requests.

Many of us operate a 'to-do' list where we scribble down tasks we need to accomplish. Certainly, this does work for many people and helps to visualize demands and needs. The feeling of crossing off something on the list seems to be so great that I've known people to write something that they've already done, just so they can cross it off and feel better!

There's no hard and fast rule about how you approach your workload, be it in your job or at home; it's about considering what works best for you. Some people need to jump in with the big-ticket items, aware that when completed they'll sail through the smaller ones. Conversely, others like to build up momentum with the smaller items to 'get into the zone' prior to rolling up their sleeves for the big numbers.

We're going to experience some situations when the demands on us clearly exceed our capacity to manage them and this may trigger feelings of fatigue, stress and overload. We'll come back to this in the next chapter on Psychological and Physical Wellbeing. In the meantime, knowing that a certain amount of juggling will be required is key to maintaining our work–life balance. Do we have a choice in this juggling? More often than not, we do, except we can't always see it that way.

A familiar trap we often fall into is to believe that everything is equally important and urgent and needs to be responded to and acted upon immediately. Our work–life balance demands usually mean this is impossible. Attempting to do everything creates a huge stress and conflict. We get frustrated or guilty if things don't fall into place and this adds to the stress further.

Marylee

When she came to see me, Marylee was totally stressed. Both her work and non-work lives demanded so much that she felt pulled in all directions. She and her husband had moved away from the connections of family and friends to find jobs in their professions. Marylee was bringing up a young family increasingly alone as her husband had to travel more, at the same time as her own job demands went stratospheric. Something had to give. Once she realized that doing everything was actually impossible, her perspective changed, and she felt more comfortable to choose what was important. After sensitively scoping it out, she realized she could take a career break and re-join when circumstances changed – for her, this was the obvious right choice.

Taking a step out of the maelstrom allows us to see things differently. Marylee's situation is not uncommon, and yet it demonstrates the battle that can emerge in our work–life balance. Things can build up and get out of hand quickly. We need to release the bubbling tension in our metaphorical pressure cooker before the lid blows off. This may require us to make some tough decisions and explore choices and their consequences.

It is widely reported that in 1954 the former US president Dwight D Eisenhower said, 'I have two kinds of demands: the urgent and the important. The urgent are rarely important and the important are rarely urgent.' Apparently, he created what is now known as the 'Eisenhower Principle' to help him prioritize and manage his workload.

Work–life balance action

The Eisenhower Principle

The Eisenhower Principle is a four-quadrant matrix (Table 4.1). Plot into each box those demands on you which are: important and urgent; important but not urgent; then urgent but not important; then not important and not urgent. I have adapted this model and continued the theme of the 'Ps' to illustrate how to act with each box, as follows:

- For what's urgent and important, prioritize them and do them first.
- Demands which are important but not urgent can be scheduled or planned to be done when your urgent and important ones have been completed.
- For the urgent but not important items, consider if you can delegate these to other people.
- Finally, for demands which are neither urgent nor important, question whether they need to be on your plan or not. Are they necessary?

Table 4.1   Eisenhower Principle matrix

	URGENT	NOT URGENT
IMPORTANT	Prioritize Do first, today	Plan Schedule for later
NOT IMPORTANT	Proxy Delegate if possible	Pass over Do you need to do this?

SOURCE Whilst Eisenhower is recognized as the originator of this model, it was popularized by Stephen R Covey in his book *The 7 Habits of Highly Effective People* (1988)

Make sure you include demands on you which cross over your work and non-work lives. Otherwise this defeats the purpose of effective planning and time management: to ensure your various commitments exist in a symbiotic harmony.

Even within the urgent/important quadrant, you may need to prioritize further. It is the plans which are not urgent/not important which often saturate our minds and create unnecessary clutter in our lives.

For our work–life balance, we might instinctively feel that entertainment or leisure activities would fit into the not urgent/not important quadrant. However, in some cases these might be important to our health and wellbeing so could be prioritized as more urgent and more important. You need to make that choice for each situation.

Delegation

Using time effectively often means recognizing the limits to what we can do on our own. Often, there's an opportunity to delegate, yet many of us struggle to do so. We may struggle to lose some control and authority handing over the baton to someone else; we might even consider that there's no one who could do the job as well as us. As we covered in Chapter 3, perfectionism is a very real threat to our work–life balance because it fixes us into an unrealistic performance trajectory which thwarts self-worth and triggers guilt and self-blame. Once we have found our way to wrestle the need to be perfect, we can realize the same applies to others too. It's important for our work–life balance to be able to let go and trust others. This might require a leap of faith but it could pay off and even exceed our own standard, as well as reduce our workload and potential burnout. We don't know until we try.

Most of us work as or in a team so we'll get asked to do things for other people, to collaborate and engage with our colleagues' work. Can we find the voice, inclination or need to do likewise? The more we delegate, the more we are likely to get our own tasks done.

The same applies in non-work situations. I can't begin to count the number of people I have worked with over the years who find it relatively straightforward to manage their work lives, including effective delegation, but fail miserably at home.

The work–life balance box exercise on page 46 in Chapter 2 concerning the family activity planner (Table 2.1), is an excellent way to delegate roles and responsibilities at home. Indeed, this can shift from an activity focus to one more functional that impacts the smooth running of the home: cleaning, vacuuming, taking the rubbish out, tidying up, laundry, ironing, shopping, cooking, repairs, etc.

One of the impediments to delegation is our anxiety that someone doesn't have the skills, competency or ability to carry out the task. In the vast majority of cases this simply requires us to identify the skills required or share our own knowledge.

A popular proverb summarizes this well: 'Give a man a fish and he will eat for a day. Teach a man to fish and he will feed for a lifetime.' The gist being that teaching someone to do something gives them the skills to take this on themselves: that is effective delegation.

This might be replicated into 'Show a colleague your spreadsheet and they'll get the figures they require. Teach them the skills of Microsoft Excel and they'll become your future report-writer.'

An alternative might be 'Show your teenager the dirty clothes basket and they'll have a tidy room for a day. Teach them to load, programme and empty the washing machine and you'll achieve domestic bliss for a lifetime.'

Benje

As an advertising account director, Benje had to meet with clients, interpret and write a creative brief, present this to the internal creative, media and planning teams before sharing the output with the client again. He took the word 'control' to a new meaning and sought to take ownership of every stage of the work process. Whilst he did have an excellent grasp of each stage, he was constantly stressed, sighing dejectedly and rubbing his forehead in exasperation. We worked on breathing and relaxation techniques initially, which helped him to enter a new calmer way of being. The big shift for him was recognizing that yes, he was in charge of the whole account but he didn't need to be in control. This realization unlocked a different perspective where he started to let go, trust and, importantly, appreciate his proficient team. He was apprehensive about delegation, but the more he tried this, the more he found he could trust others. Delegation was his biggest stress-buster.

The essence of managing involves how we work with or manage others, both at work and at home. This doesn't just involve the act of managing but extends to educating, teaching, inspiring, coaching, mentoring, encouraging and so on. We all like to learn something new. Giving a person the gift of knowing something they didn't previously will share the load further and may endear them to you.

Work–life balance action
The delegation gap

An effective means to bridge the delegation gap is simply to consider the traditional inhibitors and assess the capabilities of the individual colleague or family member. If you can answer some of the following questions, the fear of delegation is likely to recede:

What is the specific task?
Who is available and has sufficient time?
Who has the current skills or experience?
Do they really need these skills or experience?
What additional skills are required?
How can they acquire these skills or how can you teach them?
Is the task achievable in the time offered?
What might be impediments to the task completion?
What can you do to eradicate impediments?
How might you be inhibiting successful delegation or task completion?
How will you know the task has been completed sufficiently?
How will you review and assess success?

Creating a successful work–life balance relies on effective delegation. If we don't, we'll likely end up a bit like Benje in the case
study above: fraught, stressed and on the edge of meltdown.

Working hours

Benje was the first to arrive in the office and the last to leave, meaning he didn't have much time for anything else. He had a non-
existent work–life balance: his work was his life.

Though it's each person's choice how much time or effort they
put into their work lives, it's also important to not ignore the many
other wonderful experiences open to us outside of work.

In the Western world, particularly in the United States and the
UK, there is a long working-hours culture where some implicit expectation exists to 'put in the hours'. It's as if we need to be seen to
be working or justifying our presence at work. However, this takes
us back to the quality versus quantity argument I mentioned at the
beginning of this chapter.

Personally, I'd rather not be fixed to an eight hours per day employment contract but that's the norm. What if I could do my job
in, say, five hours, then get on with other aspects of my life which
contribute to my work–life balance, especially if doing so rein-
forces the quality of my five hours of 'work'? This would bring
choice back on the agenda: a collaborative choice. If my employer
could trust me to manage this, then why not? I'd put more time in
when required and take time off when not.

Perhaps it's not quite as simple as that. I genuinely do think we
all have the potential to work smarter (quality not quantity) but I
also appreciate that some employers or bosses could take advantage of that by adding to the workload further. Or we might col-
lude with the problem and simply grab more stuff to do.

Sometimes, large manufacturing organizations reduce the working week of employees when demand reduces and they need to
comparatively reduce supply. This becomes an economic decision
rather than a people decision.

Recently, a Scottish friend of mine popped back to see me one weekend, having relocated to Trondheim in Norway. Over a medicinal whisky he marvelled at the work–life balance he was now experiencing in contrast to that of the UK. In the summer, most people finished their work days by about 3pm and headed outdoors to enjoy the long, warm evenings. Many people had log cabins in the country, so spent active weekends fishing, hiking, mountain-biking, climbing, etc. There was less focus on capital accumulation, so if you didn't have a log cabin you would borrow one if it was available. No charge, just utility costs. Even in winter, whilst the nights were darker for longer, there was no expectation to work longer.

Norwegians, like in many Scandinavian countries, regard this as healthy as it reduces stress and mental ill-health. A healthier society contributes more to wider socially responsible activities and is less absent from work, which positively feeds back into the government tax coffers that in turn pays for more social care. It's an appealing cycle of sensible, pragmatic work–life balance.

In the UK at least, we have not yet learnt to embrace such forward thinking. Instead we hold on to the preoccupation with our occupation. Work rules the roost and we lose sight of what's ultimately most important to us: creating a successful work–life balance.

We often consider our working week starts on a Monday morning, but how many of us get that gnawing feeling on a Sunday evening when we start to think of the work week ahead? It might be because we are slowly cranking up the work brain cells as we prepare for what awaits us or, as is more often the case, we just start to dread getting pulled away from our home oasis and jumping back into the fast conveyor-belt pace of work.

I don't think it's unusual or that there's anything particularly wrong with being pulled back into preparing for the work day because we may need to be preparing the practical routine changes that mark the week as different from the weekend. However, if we find ourselves needlessly worrying about things that we can't do anything about at that moment, then it becomes counter-productive.

The working hours impact on work–life balance involves the judicial use of our time.

Work–life balance action

Work schedule

On the schedule in Table 4.2, map out the time spent on different activities when at work. Often, we waste much of our time with pointless meetings, idle chatter and dead-end actions. It's not to say that sometimes you might need 'down-time' but if it's 'dead-time' and serves no function, then it's poor time management. Add in a few routine activities not covered here. Ask yourself if your time could be better allocated or used.

Table 4.2   Work schedule

TASKS/ HOURS	Monday	Tuesday	Wednesday	Thursday	Friday	Total
Scheduled meetings						
Unscheduled meetings						
Professional development						
Personal development						
Phone calls						
Projects and reports						
Social conversations						
Lunch and coffee-breaks						
Administration						
Reactive responses						
Planning						

Manuela Saragosa reported in a BBC News item on 9 May 2019 that many companies have been considering the pros and cons of instituting a formal four-day working week.[1] A Glasgow-based marketing company, Pursuit Marketing, tried it and found productivity actually increased 30 per cent, sick leave dropped to an all-time low and they stumbled across further staff cost savings. However, it might not succeed everywhere. The Wellcome Trust considered and abandoned its plans due, in part, to complications regarding childcare and home arrangements, as well as anxieties about compressing work from five to four days.

There are variations on this flexible working-hours theme. My own organization, the University of Aberdeen, like many others, operates a nine-day fortnight for full-time staff. The contracted number of hours remains the same, but employees can extend their working hours for nine days to gain the tenth day off. As an added bonus to this day off, many who utilize this find that whilst initially the extended hours can seem long, they often miss the worst of commuting traffic which means less travel stress.

Having a range of flexible working opportunities might offer employees some choice to create the work–life balance they require. This also feeds back into the psychological contract discussed in Chapter 1, where our relationship with work can be central to what we put in and what we get out of it.

Present at work versus presenteeism

Most of the time, the majority of us will enjoy our work or at least derive sufficient satisfaction from it to motivate us to attend and engage with it. However, sometimes it can go the other way: we can become so work-focused that we don't pay attention to what's equally important in our wider work–life balance. If we're sniffing with a cold, experience a crisis at home or are feeling anxious or depressed, we still make it in to work. Is that really good for us or even necessary? If we consider this through our work–life balance prism, we'll see things differently.

Presenteeism is where we attend work but our productivity is reduced, largely because of ill-health; yet we struggle on. The Sainsbury Centre for Mental Health, in an undated policy document, claims that the cost of presenteeism is nearly twice the cost of sickness absence. They suggest that the cost to UK employers through absenteeism is £8.4 billion, whereas the cost attributable to presenteeism is £15.1 billion, or £605 per employee per year.[2] That's a pretty compelling rationale to re-calibrate our work–life balance.

Presenteeism tends to be defined as 'ill-health' and yet the parameters appear to stretch more widely. There's recognition that presenteeism may also be people attending work physically but who are failing to contribute to productivity. They present 'face' but little else. A proportion of this will be from ill-health but I'd argue that a significant component could be 'organizational malaise' – we're in the room but the lights are off.

There's also this strange preoccupation or fascination about being 'seen' to be busy, whether we are or not. Back in the 1980s you were not 'someone' unless you had a leather-bound Filofax bursting with papers. Nowadays the smartphone has taken over, with every call, text or message being important. Supposedly. It's like this justifies our role or makes us feel valid or important. I remember a colleague of mine from many years ago who used to dart round the office with a clipboard because it made him feel task-focused. It did surprise me that much of the time the papers on the clipboard were totally blank.

In some work environments, the pace of typing may increase, phone calls are made and people vacate the office kitchen as soon someone senior walks in. But if we have to 'seem' busy, are we using the time we do have productively?

Technology means that many people are stuck behind computer screens for much of the day and we lose that one-to-one human connection and interaction. When we surrender this people link, an important social dimension dies. I've heard of one organization that has banned e-mail communications between work colleagues when an e-mail recipient is within one minute's walk away. They're encouraging communication in the old-fashioned way: conversation. This helps employees feel more engaged and connected with their work.

Workplace stress and mental wellbeing, as key contributors to presenteeism, have a massive impact on productivity. For our own work–life balance, we need to find a way to vocalize when we're feeling ill or stressed, need to have a break or take time off if necessary. For so many reasons, this can be really difficult to talk about; many of us may find it easier to see when a colleague is struggling before we can identify it in ourselves.

I once carried out a stress-management focus group at a large financial services organization. We constructed a jigsaw-type map of all the many possible types of stressors that employees might encounter in their work and home lives. When I asked how they would identify, individually, when they were experiencing one of these stressors, there was a sea of blank faces. Yet when I asked them to pair up and identify how their work colleague might experience it, the room chatter was deafening. It's always easier to spot signs of stress in others. We spot our own signs much later down the road and usually when the damage has been done.

Pedro

Referred to me via his human resource department, Pedro came to see me with 'anger management' issues. In trying to pinpoint what was going on for him, it became apparent very quickly that he didn't actually have any anger management problems per se. He told me he was frustrated, felt undervalued and stressed at work. As we dug below the surface, at home, he was looking after his frail father and these difficult challenges at home were the main cause of his stress. With support from his human resources department, we focused on getting the elder-care support that Pedro needed. Within a few weeks, he felt much more confident about his home situation and was able to get back to his normal level of productivity at work.

The key for Pedro was being able to consider the wider picture of work–life variables, take a step back and identify changes that were required. Also crucial was his ability to ask for help and to get the support and space from his organization. Asking for help is never easy and we'll touch on this in the next chapter on Psychological and Physical Wellbeing.

Job satisfaction

If we start humming the 1965 classic from The Rolling Stones, *(I Can't Get No) Satisfaction,* on the commute to work, it's a sign that things might need to change. If we gravitate to The Clash's equally memorable 1982 classic *Should I Stay or Should I Go* then we're getting seriously close to the job-change precipice. Hopefully, we're not quite there yet but it does help us to consider and explore what constitutes job satisfaction.

I remember at the Jackie Stewart sponsors' dinner the subject of work satisfaction emerged amongst a group of us drooling over the Formula 1 Grand Prix cars. The group came out with: feeling part of a team or organization we were proud of; being able to make a difference; knowing we could continually develop and improve. We defined satisfaction as something experienced as personal and intrinsic to us. When one of the racing drivers joined us, we asked what job satisfaction meant to him: he just nodded at the cars and beamed a massive smile.

This is probably more an exception to the rule and most of us don't have the benefit of defining work satisfaction as speeding round racetracks in multimillion-pound torpedoes. The reality is that we'll have days when we're bored, naffed off, apathetic, demotivated and wondering what on earth we're doing in our jobs. I'm sure even racing drivers have their boring days too.

Satisfaction needs to contain components of three derivatives. We need some form of *validation* which generates an approval by others or the self of something we have achieved. This is created by knowing, at some level, that we are acknowledged for what we do, through appreciation or financial recompense. We also need to feel some sense of *fulfilment* that allows us to experience a completeness or resolution. This is achieved by 'getting a job done' or doing so within the terms originally set out. Finally, we need to experience a *feel-good factor*: a result which makes us feel buoyant, upbeat or pleased with our efforts.

You might read this and revert back to humming *(I Can't Get No) Satisfaction* but life at work, or home for that matter, is never going to generate 100 per cent satisfaction. It's not only impossible but it's also undesirable.

If we break down the components of satisfaction above (validation, fulfilment and a feel-good factor) then, by definition, these can only exist as we work towards achieving them. Most things in life which constitute an achievement require effort and graft. If everything is easy and requires minimal effort, then the achievement or satisfaction would feel hollow and muted.

Job satisfaction is an important component of our work–life balance repertoire because it contributes to purpose and meaning at work, as discussed in Chapter 1, as well as the more day-to-day motivation for getting us up in the morning and attending to our jobs.

Miranda

At the top of her game, Miranda was a senior politician in her party, respected by many on all sides of government. She had a passionate belief in serving her political party and what this represented. She was on various committees and think-tanks, contributing to policy development and strategy. She came to me puzzled about her apparent drop in motivation and inspiration. Eventually we deduced that this was connected with the fact that her party was way ahead in the polls and likely to win a new term in government. What was missing was what she'd loved before: being the underdog in opposition, battling to win the prize of being in government. Now she was there, her chief driver and motivator had gone. It was, to her, a bit boring now. Once she recognized this shift in motivation, she was able to re-jig her aspirations to maintaining her position in government. This still required her to fight her corner and battle to sustain what she had achieved.

With other clients I have worked with on similar job satisfaction issues, what appeared to help was to simply keep a daily log of whether a day was 'good' or 'bad' and, importantly, why. This can often reveal an important, emerging unease or discomfort. Once we know what the thorn is, we can start to identify how we can address it. Often it's things that happen which generate frustration or where we have lost our limited control over the process or outcome. Circumstances occur in spite of us, not necessarily because of us. Even with the best planning or preparation, we can't anticipate every eventuality.

Work–life balance action
Job satisfaction

If you can identify what parts of your job satisfy you, then it makes sense to take efforts to protect this or generate more. If you experience some underlying dissatisfaction but are not clear about this, it might help to speak with a coach or counsellor. If you do have a rough idea what the problem is then you're half-way to working around potential solutions or resolutions.

Have a think about the statements in Table 4.3 and add in your own.

Identifying a source of discontent and exploring solutions has a significant impact on work–life balance as it has the potential to re-energize and stimulate us in our work domain.

Table 4.3 Job satisfaction

	YES – how can you enhance this?	NO – what might be solutions?
I know what is expected of me		
I have the skills to do my job		
My workload is about right		

(continued)

Table 4.3 (Continued)

	YES – how can you enhance this?	NO – what might be solutions?
I can manage stress and pressure		
I am satisfied with my job		
I have enough control in my role		
I am supported sufficiently		
I have adequate resources		
I am motivated and inspired		
I have good work relationships		
I have time to do what is required		
I have a good work–life balance		

Delay gratification

Connected with how we define and experience job satisfaction is how we deal with self-control and expectations surrounding this.

In the 1960s and '70s, Stanford psychologist Walter Mischel conducted the infamous 'marshmallow test' with 90 children.[3] This involved a researcher offering a child one marshmallow immediately or two if they waited 15 minutes. About 30 per cent of the children waited the 15 minutes. A decade or so later Mischel reviewed the development of these children and claimed that those who had waited the 15 minutes exhibited greater self-control and life satisfaction as well as overall educational advancement.

Whilst this research has been challenged since, it still bears currency today simply because it makes sense. In our fast-paced society, we want everything immediately. The savouring and anticipation is lost. We can buy almost anything online at the click of a button. The only time-lag involves searching through what can feel like thousands of web pages first. In doing so, we lose some of the experience.

The notion of self-control is important for how we manage expectations of ourselves and others. It is relevant to work–life balance as it creates a stronger sense of perspective in our worlds. The more we work, or wait, for something, the greater the achievement we experience.

In Scotland, mountains over 3,000 feet are called Munros, named after Sir Hugh Munro, who listed the peaks which reached that threshold. Thousands of intrepid hill walkers trudge their way up these hills so they can claim to have 'bagged a Munro'. It has become a quest for many to bag all 282 of them and even to compete over the number of times they climb them all. As I have recently achieved my fiftieth over some 40 years, I doubt I'll be one of them but it would make a lovely work–life balance ambition.

Munro-baggers, as they are called, demonstrate the essence of delaying gratification and illustrate that whilst the goal is to reach the top, the enjoyment and experience is in the journey to get there. There's no better feeling after a six-hour climb, often in rather inclement weather conditions, than reaching the peak and, as tradition determines, either kissing the cairn (peak marker) or adding a stone to the mound at the top. It wouldn't generate anything like the achievement that it feels without the time and effort put into getting there.

We don't need to forge through rain and sleet to experience the journey of achievement. Work–life balance likewise includes putting some effort into the things we come to enjoy, savour and appreciate in life. It's about choosing how we use our time and what we get out of this.

As a teenager in the 1980s, I had this dream of owning a Porsche 911 Targa. At that time, I didn't have the disposable income to splash out on such an extravagance. So I said to myself that I would treat myself and buy one when I reached the age of 40. That was a serious 22-year delay of gratification, but being reminded of my aim over the decades would rekindle my enthusiasm, and also

helped to alleviate any anticipated anxiety about any 'mid-life crisis' (which, as it happened, failed to materialize).

What did I do when I reached 40? I didn't buy a Porsche. Instead,
I took my motorbike licence and soon biked my way, on a beast of
a machine, through some stunningly beautiful routes in the Scottish
Highlands. It was great fun, and knowing I'd had a choice between
two fantastic opportunities was amazing. However, the cost to me
was the hill walking I'd otherwise have enjoyed at the same time. I
realized that this had given me more satisfaction… and was somewhat healthier to body and planet. In the end, for my own work–
life balance, I chose to ditch the bike and revert back to hill walking.
Who knows, I might still buy a Porsche one day, but at the moment, I don't think it would improve my work–life balance.

As we've seen, much of creating a successful work–life balance
is making choices, some of them tough. Gratification delay or self-
control allows us to prioritize activities and demands so that we
become judicious about time management. This doesn't mean we
can't have down-time or treats but it needs to be within the grand
scheme of things.

Greg

Like many of us, Greg struggled to juggle the demands of home and
work. He felt he never really had quality time on his own. When we
reviewed his 'down-time' opportunities, we recognized that he did in
fact have routine slots in his day when he could recharge his batteries.
However, he tended to while this away 'gaming', spooling through
social media or watching comedy clips on YouTube. Greg chose to
change this and build into his day more definitive and enriching
experiences, including walking his neighbour's dog after work and
listening to online guided meditation tracks before he went to sleep. He
proposed to limit gaming to weekends. Even though he considered it a
tough call to do this, he recognized with some excitement how much
more he would enjoy it this way. For Greg, less was more.

Personal efficiency

Focusing is very much a process which we can practise and develop. For our work–life balance it means we are able to inject the appropriate level of concentration to attend to the task in the best way in the quickest time. This is about personal efficiency. Why spend longer doing something when we don't have to?

Some of us are skilled at multitasking: attending to several demands at the same time. This is usually perceived as being something that's hard-wired in our brains, but I would argue that it can actually evolve in us, due to necessity. Parents with children often speak about juggling the needs of the family and home by shifting from one activity or demand to another in short succession.

I'm always amazed and somewhat jealous of people who can type away into their computer whilst holding a telephone conversation with someone on a totally different subject. I can't even write and talk at the same time, at least not in any meaningful way.

Work–life balance action
Multitasking

This is a light-hearted, fun activity to test your multitasking skills. Get a partner and both stand up facing each other. Start a conversation about something with which you are both familiar. Then gently pat your head with your left hand, whilst circling your stomach with the right hand. Do this to the count of five, then swap round, tapping your head with the right hand and circling your stomach with the left hand. Keep going for 10 repetitions, swapping your hands each time.

In a completely unscientific experiment with six friends who came round for dinner a few weeks ago, only two of them (not me) completed this activity correctly to the end. The couple who already knew they could multitask were the winners.

However, I am determined to improve on this and have started practising this routine in my door-closed office at work. I am getting better at this: it can be learnt. I'm just hoping I'm not disturbed because it's going to take some explaining with me talking to myself as I pat my head and rub my stomach!

Whether we multitask or not, the key is being able to give sufficient attention, concentration and focus to the intended activity. As with Greg above, we may have to make choices about what we do, how and when.

Procrastination

We've all experienced that annoying, frustrating and nagging feeling when we're not doing something we know we should. We can't be bothered, we have excuses, we are preoccupied elsewhere or we believe it's not important to do right now. Many reasons for procrastinating involve not having the tools, information, knowledge or resources at hand.

Many of my clients over the years have found that procrastination involves not knowing where or how to start. There's also the link into perfectionism, discussed previously, where our quest to perform a task perfectly makes us realize that we might not be able to do so. In this way we feel it is better not to start, rather than attempt a task half-heartedly.

The simple way to get rid of procrastination is to start doing something; *anything*. It is inactivity and inaction that perpetuate and feed procrastination.

Chen

As an aspiring screenwriter, Chen would spend much of his day evolving characters, plot-lines, dramatic sequences and story structures. Yet even with a number of scripts under his belt, he would still suffer writer's block, as he would call it. Our simple yet effective remedy was that when he experienced this void, he would type out into his laptop a Robert Burns poem from a book he owned and loved. Then he would recite the poem. You could choose anything but the point here was that Chen would need to concentrate on copying old Scots language and crafting appropriate stanza layout. By reading it out he'd be rewarding himself for his efforts, particularly as he was from South Korea and English was his second language. Both efforts required him to focus and get his brain engaged in the task. The fact he was writing was also starting up the writing focus. This method consistently got rid of his writer's block.

What Chen was doing was broadly following the sequence of tips that often help to get rid of procrastination. His work–life balance was significantly improved because he got more done without the stressful tension of struggling with his block and getting started.

Work–life balance action
Avoiding procrastination

The following tips can help you work through procrastination. Tick off each one as you achieve it:

- ☐ Avoid distractions – turn off the internet, silence your mobile and text or e-mail alerts.

- ☐ Allocate a specific amount of time with a clear start- and end-point.

- ☐ Plan, schedule and prioritize – most activities require as much planning as execution.

- ☐ Identify any knowledge gaps – find out what information is missing and where to get it.

- ☐ Delegate or collaborate – it can help to speak to others to get you focused and 'in the zone'.

- ☐ Break your work down into steps, so they don't feel so big.

☐ Create specific and achievable mini-goals.

☐ Visualize the results, how you get from A through to B and how you'll feel when completed.

☐ Find a way to enjoy the work ahead and why you're doing what you're doing.

☐ Give yourself a reward for each achievement or goal accomplished (delay gratification).

Often we struggle to create a successful work–life balance because of wasted or poorly used time. Have a look back at the work schedule you completed in Table 4.2 on page 112: if you look back over the last week, I guarantee that you will be able to identify slots of 'dead' time. The challenge is to learn from this and get more out of life.

Each of us has our own capacity for focusing and concentration. We need to find what suits us. If we work flat out for too long we might get tired and lose our edge. Alternatively, we might develop physical discomfort from over-long periods of sitting or repetitive actions.

One method which I have found helpful for my clients is to adopt what's called the Pomodoro Technique for creating dedicated chunks of focused work time. This was developed by Francesco Cirillo in the 1980s.[4] The idea is to work in blocks of 25 minutes, aided by a timing device, or clock, which you can set for 25 minutes before it rings or the alarm kicks in. Then you take a 5-minute break where you do something to refresh or recharge your mind. Ideas include taking a short walk, carrying out breathing or mindfulness exercises, making a coffee or drinking water and so on. Then you get back into another 25-minute cycle. After four blocks of 25 plus 5 minutes, take a longer 15- or 20-minute break.

This method works well as it creates shorter work-time spells and builds in frequent mini-breaks. It reduces the potential for overload and yet it gives adequate time to get into a task.

Flow state

Can you think of a time when you were so engrossed or absorbed in an activity that you lost all sense of time or how long you'd been at it? This is commonly referred to as being in a state of 'flow' and was championed in a book of the same name in 1990 by psychologist Mihaly Csikszentmihalyi.[5]

Flow is the opposite to feelings of apathy and boredom because in these states we are not challenged. When we have an ability to stretch our skills or competencies and experience a challenge, we're likely to find ourselves in a learning and focusing zone. Optimal experiences therefore emerge when we are engaged at a high-skill and high-challenge level. The absence of either of these levels will prevent us getting into the flow state.

This presents us with the opportunity to find tasks or activities that stretch our abilities and present a sufficient challenge at the same time. Admittedly, we're not always going to have the opportunity of achieving this but it is possible to seek out tasks with this intentionality.

Managing ambition

What does ambition mean to you? Is it an important part of your personal and professional development or do you feel some societal, family or even parental pressure to demonstrate your worth? Are you looking for external validation, ie adoration, praise or approval of others? We all like to know we're doing well at our work but how can we best monitor or recognize this?

Perhaps our ambition relates to developing our personal relationships, raising a family, being part of the community, becoming more engaged in non-work activities. Ambition doesn't have to be limited to our work lives.

We close this chapter with an important focus on managing ambition. This might sit in the background yet can be a strong motivator for our current and future productivity and performance.

Most of us only revise our curriculum vitae or resumé when we're actively looking for a new job. It's worth updating this on a regular interval so that we're adding achievements as we go along. Often when it comes to the crunch, we've forgotten about some of the big triumphs which can make relevant and useful reading for a recruiter.

Regularly updating a CV can also reveal any experience or skills that we want to or may need to gain; at any stage in the job cycle, we have a potential to develop and advance. This might be within our current organization or perhaps it needs to be in a new one. Where are you now and where do you want to be in the future? One of the crucial questions is 'why?' Is it because we want better remuneration or take on greater responsibility? In some cases, we might be perfectly satisfied with where we are but we want further challenges.

In both a work and non-work context, ambition can get caught up with competitiveness. Maybe we still hang out with our friends of old and there's still a competitive streak underlying these relationships, or the same might apply with sibling rivalry. We want to prove ourselves, we want to prove our worth. But why is this necessary and what does this actually prove at the end of the day?

This is not to undermine the importance or relevance of ambition but more an encouragement to consider the motives for ambition and how this impacts work–life balance. How might this impact our partner, family and friends? How could this threaten established aspects of a current successful work–life balance? Sometimes we might experience a push/pull factor: either an enthusiastic inclination to jump up to the next stage of life or a feeling of being dragged reluctantly into a new pathway because we 'should'.

A job might be creating discomfort but it's worth considering if, or the degree to which, we might be colluding with the problem. Is there something we can be doing differently or better that will change our experience?

Brock

Whilst performing satisfactorily in his job, Brock was getting frustrated at work and said he wanted to get on, get out and get up the corporate ladder elsewhere. As we explored his drives, motivations and ambitions, we realized his current job was a perfect fit. The problem was in his own behaviour in that he had got into a dysfunctional habit of moaning about what he did, venting frustrations and generally moping around. There wasn't actually anything wrong with him or the work, but he'd fallen into this negative mentality due to familiarity with his work. He realized there still was challenge, excitement and opportunity. He had become his own psychological block. Once he made the conscious effort to adopt a more positive demeanour and adapt his mindset, everything started to fall back into shape again.

Ambition and moving onwards in our career can be tremendously exciting, but it could also create some anxiety and tension because we just don't know how things will pan out. Getting allies or our 'dream team' on board to help steer us in the right direction can mitigate some of this pressure.

It can be difficult to know when to 'make the move'. Some people just seem to judge the timing right, others might find they have stayed too long in one role or left too early. There's no rule here as all of our circumstances are different. It's about being able to reflect in a considered manner and especially with an eye on how this might impact our work–life balance.

There's also no real end-point with ambition. Why not reach for the stars? I had an engineering friend who would always go on about aiming to work for NASA (National Aeronautics and Space Administration). I admit to being somewhat flippant and sceptical about this and had no sense that this was ever going to happen. Except it did. Not only did he reach for the stars but he got a job closely associated with them.

Anything can happen. However, because of a poorly scheduled ambition in my own work–life balance, my quest to becoming fluent in Portuguese feels increasingly less likely. Instead, maybe I should contact NASA?

The MARTYR Principle

A key threat to a successful work–life balance is not completing what we set out or hope to achieve. In this way we are occupied by loose ends or generate feelings of frustration or stress. Little things left incomplete can take up a lot of head space, worry and anxiety. All that is required is to adopt a more systematic approach to getting things done.

Tasks or goals have a greater chance of success if we have the conditions to succeed in them. These can be applied to both home and work lives by simply following a procedure I have evolved, called the MARTYR Principle. You can remember this by the notion of 'not being a martyr to your goals'.

Work–life balance action
The MARTYR Principle

The MARTYR Principle can help you start and finish goals or tasks:

M Goals need to be **measurable** with a start- and end-point with paced-out stepping stones

A Goals should be **achievable** in relation to your skills, resources and time available

R Goals should be **realistic** and capable of being completed sufficiently well

T Plan and schedule adequate **time** with some contingency

Y You must **yearn** to want to complete the task: enthusiasm creates energy and action

R Build in a **reward**, appreciation or acknowledgement of the goal achievement

---

'Get a Life' needs audit scaling system: productivity and performance

The scaling system in the table below applies for each section discussed in this chapter and is based on your personal perception of whether there is a deficiency, imbalance or need... or not. Everyone is different so there's no right or wrong. This simply allows you to consider the gaps that exist for you.

The scoring uses a self-rating percentage index from 0–100 with 0 per cent referring to needs totally **unmet** and 100 per cent equating to needs totally **met**. Add up the percentage totals and divide this by the number of sections to give you a total percentage for this chapter. At the end of the book, you will have a percentage total for each chapter giving you scope to consider where you need to prioritize action.

If any sections are irrelevant to you, ignore them and reduce the number of sections you divide this by accordingly.

	Sections	Percentage of needs currently met %
1	Time management	
2	Delegation	
3	Working hours	
4	Job satisfaction	
5	Personal efficiency	
6	Managing ambition	
Total Score for Chapter 4 (out of 600%): Productivity and Performance		
Divide this Total Score by **6**		
Total Percentage Score (out of 100%) for Chapter 4		

Figure 4.1   Productivity and performance needs audit radar

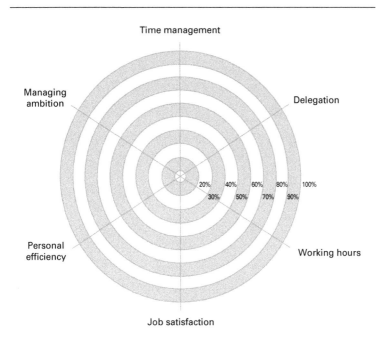

For the more visually minded, plot a dot on the radar diagram (Figure 4.1) with the same percentage scale: 0 for needs totally unmet up to 100 per cent for needs totally met. You can then join the dots together to form a needs audit radar. This method gives you a visual cue to identify the gaps in your needs.

This chapter on Productivity and Performance has focused on the more functional and practical minutiae of how we perform at work and how to improve our effectiveness and efficiency. Working faster and smarter allows us to choose how best to use the demands on our time. Whilst much of the focus has been directed to our work lives, we have seen that our non-work lives also benefit from efficient planning and scheduling of our time.

The next chapter recognizes that with the best work–life juggling skills in the world, our Psychological and Physical Wellbeing ultimately determines the scope and feasibility of what our minds and bodies can cope with and need.

Endnotes

1 Saragosa, M (2019) Could your firm move to a four-day week?, BBC News Business, 5 May. Available from: www.bbc.co.uk/news/business-48125411 (archived at https://perma.cc/T7AS-ESJK)
2 Sainsbury Centre for Mental Health (nd) *Mental Health at Work: Developing the business case,* Policy Paper 8, Sainsbury Centre for Mental Health, London
3 Mischel, W (2014) *The Marshmallow Test: Understanding self-control and how to master it,* Penguin Random House, London
4 Cirillo, F (nd) The Pomodoro Technique. Available at francescocirillo.com/pages/pomodoro-technique (archived at https://perma.cc/69GS-X277)
5 Csikszentmihalyi, M (1990) *Flow: The psychology of optimal experience,* Harper & Row Publishers, New York

05
Psychological and physical wellbeing

Much of what has been discussed so far has involved our work or home environments. They are external or extrinsic in that we dip in and out of these locations according to our demands and schedule. They can also change; we might move house, begin or end relationships or transition into a different job. What remains constant though is that we remain the same person throughout. We will evolve, learn and develop but we're stuck with the bodies and minds that make us who we are.

Our character, identity and personality will significantly shape the way we create and manage our work–life balance. We're all influenced by a multitude of factors, life events and experiences. Our upbringing, parents and friends will have impacted on relationships and communication skills, all of which blend into how we get on with people around us.

Maintaining our physical and mental health as part of our work–life balance will all be influenced by these unique factors.

Stress management

We all need a certain amount of pressure in our lives to give us motivation and challenge. Unfortunately, maintaining a healthy work–life balance is not straightforward. We can't determine the pace, speed or sequence of demands on us, however well-organized we are. Things change and when pressure mounts up on us we need to deal with it. The Eisenhower Principle covered in Chapter 4 on page 106 highlighted that we may have some control over what we decide is important or urgent in terms of priorities. Sometimes, however, everything seems urgent and important.

If we find ourselves with more demands than we can reasonably cope with, we can feel like a pressure cooker: close to boiling point. Something has to give. We need to release some of that pressure before the situation becomes overwhelming.

As pressure mounts, it can be difficult to maintain a sense of perspective because we become tunnel-visioned. Our resources are spent tackling demands rather than taking a step back to ease some of that pressure. If we are in high-pressure mode for a short period of time, it's likely we may cope just fine. This is what helps to define a personal resilience, as we learn to cope with adverse pressure. The key is being able to identify the point at which this lasts longer than we can cope with or when we are getting close to overload and burnout.

Stress is a term to describe the point at which our coping and managing skills become insufficient to deal with the pressures put upon us. The Human Performance Curve (see Figure 5.1) is linked to the Yerkes–Dodson law, devised by psychologists Robert Yerkes and John Dodson in 1908 to illustrate that performance increases in proportion to stress or arousal, but only to a point. Excess stress or arousal reduces performance.[1]

Ideally, we need to be operating at the engaged/motivated pace. Below this we can become apathetic or inactive, beyond which we tire or burn out. The tricky bit is working out what works for us. A *motivated* point to you might feel like a *burnout* point to me or vice versa.

From a work–life balance point of view, some of us may be better able to deal with pressures in one particular sphere of our lives, be it work or home. This may be because one is more familiar or we have boundaries or limits in place. We may have better support and resources too. It's true to say though that we might also feel unable to cope in any or all segments of life. We don't necessarily forge an inbuilt stress barometer. School equips us with an education but not necessarily how to cope with the pressures of life.

Figure 5.1 Human Performance Curve adapted from Yerkes–Dodson (1908)

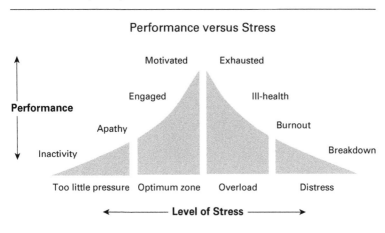

Performance versus Stress

We have probably all felt 'stressed' at some point in life, which will have invariably impacted our work–life balance. We are not immune to life events or tough and difficult situations.

Konstance

After losing her father from a lengthy battle with cancer, Konstance found her home life greatly impacted by the loss. The family was more present, as were memories from photos and letters. She was grieving and took time to appreciate the normal, if distressing, aspects of loss. She found work much easier to cope with as her job, as a credit controller, required her to focus and concentrate. This gave her boundaries and a structure within which she could get on with her life.

I met with her a few times as she felt this imbalance was insensitive or 'wrong'. She felt she should be grieving in all aspects of her life. However, in time she realized that work was an important calibrating environment, giving some temporary respite time away from grieving. It gave her permission to put the loss 'on hold' for part of her day and so to function better.

The impact of life events or the build-up of stress can affect us in a myriad of different ways. For Konstance, she was unaccustomed to loss, especially of someone so close. Her familiar ways of coping were not sufficient to enable her to understand and appreciate the uniqueness of her situation and what was, in fact, OK.

Richard

When I met Richard, he presented with anger management issues. He felt he was losing control over how he was handling a spate of stressful situations. He would often snap at his family and work colleagues. Each time he calmed down, he felt guilty and remorseful. Richard wanted to know about stress-management techniques so he could find alternatives to his anger outbursts. Whilst we did explore some relaxation and breathing exercises, he realized it was also helpful to learn about himself and his stress triggers. If he could identify when the stress was moving from his motivated and optimum level to one that touched into exhaustion and overload, he could take steps to prevent any adverse behavioural reaction.

As Richard found, it is much better to manage stress pre-emptively rather than in the heat of the moment. This does require a conscious effort and some practice. As I mentioned in Chapter 4, it's often easier to spot signs of stress in a family member or work colleague than it is to identify it in ourselves. When I last gave a workshop on stress, I asked the audience to raise their hands if they could identify when they were becoming stressed. A smattering of hands rose. When I asked if they had recently spotted signs of stress in any of their colleagues, they pretty much all raised their hands, pointing at each other, smiling and nodding.

Our work–life balance can be much better calibrated when we anticipate and act on potential feelings of stress *before* they move into overload zone. In response to this, I developed an ABCDE

Stress Trigger Indicator to help us all spot signs of stress in ourselves and others. If we can better spot signs of stress, we have the opportunity to look after and look out for each other.

***

Work–life balance action
ABCDE stress trigger indicator

If you identify with any of the stress triggers below, you or your family member or work colleague may be experiencing symptoms of stress. The ABCDE covers:

- **A**ffective – feelings and emotions;
- **B**ehavioural – actions;
- **C**ognitive – thoughts and reasoning;
- **D**ifferences – changes;
- **E**nvironmental – social.

This covers the more common triggers, and terms have been chosen for their commonality rather than necessarily being an accurate fit into a category, because there is some overlap, shown in Table 5.1.

***

A common theme from the above is to notice changes: changes in how we think, behave or act. We tend to function with fairly consistent habits, so it is when we deviate from our norm that things might be adversely affecting us and generating stress.

Positive thinking

A major inhibitor to work–life balance is dysfunctional thinking which can unnecessarily skew the way we interpret and process our experience of life. Are we colluding with what might otherwise be a more positive perspective? Effective work–life balance is about

Table 5.1 ABCDE stress trigger indicator

Affective/emotional	Behavioural/actions	Cognitive/thoughts	Differences	Environmental
Anxiety/tension	Erratic behaviour	Over-worrying	Appetite changes	Avoiding people
Irritation/angst	Sleep pattern changes	Depression/low mood	Weight gain/loss	Increased socialization
Anger/aggression	Sweating/palpitations	Negative thinking	Exercise changes	Increased alcohol
Frustration/annoyance	Unusual behaviour	Lack of perspective	Jitters/flushes	Rebellious
Moodiness	Disorganized	Disorganized/erratic	Back/neck pain	Mistrustful
Panic attacks	Argumentative	Poor decision-making	Cold sweat/shakes	Home/work apathy
Impatience	Aggressive driving	Increased mistakes	Skin conditions	Excessive shopping
Tearful	Lack of energy	Poor concentration	Migraine/headaches	Work absences
Restless/fidgety	Absent-minded	Obsessiveness	Nail-biting/hair-pulling	Avoiding hobbies
Uneasy/uncertain	Late into work	Neuroticism	Forgetful	Increased risk-taking

enjoying all aspects of our busy lives as much as possible. Admittedly, we're all going to have off-days or experience a life crisis event along the way, so it is impossible to be thinking positively all the time.

I like to regard positive thinking as 'not negative thinking'. It might seem like a double negative, but I've found with clients over the years that when you reduce or minimize negative thinking you open up a more instinctive flow of positive thinking. It just naturally emerges. Negative thinking can be likened to the anchor of a boat. When it's engaged, we don't go anywhere; we're stationary and stuck. But when disengaged, we can sail unrestricted into the distant sunset. We always have the potential to drop our anchor during tough times but we do have some choice over whether we let it drop or not.

Encouraging a positive thinking mentality can be difficult if there's a backdrop of negative thinking. It doesn't matter how many fancy engines we have on our boat, it still won't go anywhere if the anchor's down.

There's an important distinction here though. Some crucial emotions exist to help us cope with difficult situations. It's OK to feel sad when we experience loss, disappointment when something doesn't work out as planned, or regret if we have acted inappropriately. This emotional barometer allows us to express how we feel in relation to a myriad of experiences. It's important for our health and wellbeing, though, for these emotions to be proportionate to the situation and temporary. If we find ourselves mired in long-term sadness, disappointment or regret, this might indicate the potential benefit in speaking to a therapist or coach.

Work–life balance action
Negative thinking

The following presents a summary of common negative-thinking traits. Can you identify with any of them?

Biased blame	Taking responsibility for something you weren't to blame for or not taking responsibility for something you were

Catastrophizing	Blowing things out of proportion or seeing the worst-case scenario
Conditionality	Seeing things in absolute terms: 'I do something perfectly or I'm useless'
Negative bias	Only looking at the negative evidence and not the positives
Generalizing	Making general conclusions with only limited evidence
Critical words	Being influenced by opinionated words like 'should' or 'must'
Emotionality	Being led by how we feel to determine how we think ie sad means bad
Future bias	Assuming the future will be tarred by difficult times from the past
Past block	Failing to live in the present by being held back by past experiences
Assumptions	Believing we know how others will act, feel or think without real evidence

Recognizing some of the negative scripts in our lives is the first step to challenging and changing them. Some can be associated with significant past life events or experiences and may not be easily shifted. That's not to say they can't be. Rather, it may require the intervention of a therapist or coach to help find the way through.

The categories of the ABCDE stress trigger indicator discussed earlier can offer a doorway for changing negative thinking. Each of the areas can be interconnected, potentially influencing each other. This means that skewed thinking habits can be altered by triggering a change to our feelings, moods and emotions, our actions or behaviours, attending to a physical difference or engaging with our social or wider environment.

Alternatively, a popular way of re-appraising negativity is to consider the evidence for or against any automatic negative thoughts. Re-evaluating the emotions or feelings associated with the negative thoughts can change the interpretation of a situation.

Once we make a conscious effort to reduce habits of negativity, we will experience a range of positive outcomes, all of which will impact work–life balance. Negativity takes up so much headspace and creates a repetitive spiral that rarely goes anywhere. Freeing this up allows us to make more rational choices about our needs and demands in work and home lives. Basically, it means we'll enjoy more from our lives. Who doesn't want that?

Calmness from anxiety and worry

Decisions and choices made with a clear, uncluttered head are likely to generate a better outcome because we will be more pro-ductive and decisive, and less prone to mistakes or accidents. Major obstacles to this, and especially to the maintenance of a successful work–life balance, are anxiety and worry.

There's nothing wrong with or bad about anxiety per se and we can all be affected by it. It is an important primal emotion which, in evolutionary terms, alerts us to signs of danger. We could choose to fight, take flight or freeze in response to this threat. However, the degree to which we experience anxiety may sometimes be mis-placed and out of proportion to the threat. We can also get into a habit of finding threat in almost anything we do. This is aligned to negative thinking patterns where we settle into a well-worn famili-arity of being an anxious person, and in turn results in unnecessary wasted time, distress and tension.

Much anxiety or worry emerges because we don't know what an outcome might be or we fear the worst. Often, the fear of uncertainty or not knowing conjures up the dread. Life doesn't give us the luxury of knowing everything or predicting what will happen. We need to find a way to tolerate ambiguity and uncertainty.

Milo

When he came to see me, Milo was visibly anxious. He was three weeks away from learning whether he had been successfully awarded his PhD. He just couldn't stand the wait and was fearing all manner of negative consequences if he didn't get it. After years of hard graft and significant debt, he was fearing the worst; letting down his academic supervisor, that he'd never get a job, his wife and family would disown him and all his friends would think he was a fraud.

We challenged the evidence. He had to wait three weeks for his results and there was nothing he could do to change that. Fact. Everything else, not fact. He could control how he coped with the wait by attending to changes in how he thought, felt and acted towards it. We went through the ABCDE model and he chose a number of actions: routinely practise the mindfulness body scan to relax more (affective);[2] leave his home for a period of time during the day (behavioural); do something physical (differences); and engage with others (environmental/social) by volunteering for 10 days with a working party cleaning a beach on the west coast of Scotland.

When he contacted me to tell me of his PhD achievement, Milo was at pains to highlight the intense fun he'd had with his beach-cleaning experience, with the added bonus of gaining a couple of new friends. To me, this was a massive work–life balance result.

As we consider the impact of anxiety and worry on our work–life balance, the key is taking action. Inaction is the feeder for anxiety. As the popular saying goes: 'If you do what you've always done (worry), you'll get what you've always got (worry).' If we always dread a public-speaking engagement with fear and hysteria, then each time we're faced with a public-speaking engagement, we'll probably experience a mix of fear and hysteria. Something has to change and stop this cycle.

I've used a simple model over the years, which can help dispel the myths of our worries and so achieve a sense of calmness. The source of this is unknown. I call it the 'Don't worry, be happy' model.

Work–life balance action
Don't worry, be happy

The 'Don't worry, be happy' model really challenges us to consider the point or purpose of why and when we worry. If we can do something about what worries us then we are taking control and doing something to mitigate and reduce the need to worry. If we can't do anything about it, then worrying about it isn't going to help (Figure 5.2). This introduces a choice component to the preoccupation of worrying – we can choose to worry or choose not to worry.

Figure 5.2   The 'Don't worry, be happy' model

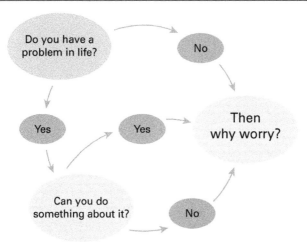

The 'be happy' part of the model essentially means that by getting rid of the worry we open ourselves up to the opportunity of happiness and calmness. It's difficult to worry and be truly happy at the same time.

Katy

When her husband lost his job, Katy needed to find one after many years looking after the home. She took a role at a small conference centre managing the cleaning and catering staff. It was something with which she had prior experience, but she became, as she described to me, a 'professional worrier', fretting and panicking about almost every aspect of her role. When we applied the 'Don't worry, be happy' model, she began to realize that this had become her habitual way of being: there was actually not much she needed to worry about. As soon as she realized this was unnecessary and served no functional purpose, she recognized the opportunities for change. Furthermore, the calmness she experienced by parking her worrying behaviour meant her job satisfaction significantly increased.

Become resilient by facing your fears

Anxiety and worry can be significant inhibitors to effective work–life balance because they act as stalling blocks. We become more paralysed by the anxiety than the anxiety trigger itself. Spending time fretting over an upcoming event – such as a public-speaking engagement – may reduce our focus and ability to prepare for it, causing even greater anxiety. On the other hand, if we hold with the belief that we'll do well, we're more likely to put on a good performance. If we believe we can achieve something, we probably will. Self-belief and trust in oneself can become a significant accelerator for success.

As it happens, a fear of failure is often greater than the experience or consequence of the failure. Resilience comes from accepting we will encounter difficult circumstances but that we have the capacity to learn and adapt from these. By doing this, we become more flexible, better prepared for and immunized against the destructive impacts of challenging future life events.

This all involves a mindset of not running away from the things that make us anxious or worried. It's about facing them. What's achieved by running away from a fear? The fear will remain. Somehow we must find a way to understand it, make sense of it and de-escalate the fear component.

It's important to recognize there is good fear and anxiety, just like there are good bacteria in our bodies to maintain health and help us function. Good fear and anxiety warns us of real danger and significant threats. We should assess where this 'real' component exists. When I was young, I learnt a valuable lesson about not setting alight a pile of leaves in the garden with petrol. My fear of petrol fire is real and commensurate with the risks involved. No more petrol on leaves.

However, my anxiety about filming my first live podcast was not the same as this petrol fear. My life would not face the same prospect of death. It was a performance anxiety and partly related to the unfamiliar podcast format. Facing this fear, I realized this anxiety was good. It made me prepare, practise and research. I was alert and 'on the ball'. It went brilliantly and I felt really good afterwards. I had faced this fear and survived. In fact, not only did I survive but it helped inspire me further. If we successfully quash a quashable fear, then we're likely to feel exhilarated by it. It can make us realize that once we vanquish a fear, we are stronger and more capable than we think. When we believe we can handle almost anything that comes our way, we'll be in a better position to take risks and blossom our creativity. We can live the life we deserve. As the German philosopher, Friedrich Nietzsche, claimed, 'That which does not kill us, makes us stronger.'[3]

Facing the fear with resilience is about not being threatened with self-judgement and self-doubt. This reflects back to the negative-thinking conundrum discussed earlier in this chapter. You're not a failure if you don't achieve what you aim for; you're a success because you tried. Resilience involves bouncing back from difficult situations, which requires in us a capacity to leap forward from adversity. If you take the image of a javelin thrower – they have to pull back in order to propel it forward. Sometimes we might need to take one step back in order to achieve two steps forwards.

As I've mentioned previously, fears and anxieties often exist because of an unknown component. We just don't have enough information available to authenticate or assess the fear. Once we have better insight or information we are better able to rationalize and adjudicate the actual fear. Sometimes, though, we're not going to have sufficient information in the moment and we simply need to go out, face it and deal with it.

From a work–life balance perspective, take the example of an annual extended-family gathering which might normally present you with tension or anxiety. OK, maybe last year's event created some conflicts, but it doesn't mean it will be the same this year. There could have been tensions between a couple of relatives but that was their issue, not yours. Some people were late, others didn't turn up. Last year was last year. This year is a new experience. Face this anxiety and already the prospect will change for you.

Another scenario might involve being called into an unplanned meeting with your boss. You might think – what have I done wrong, why me, am I getting fired? Or you could choose to think: 'I have no idea what the meeting is about so there's no point worrying about it. I will choose to stay calm and accept whatever comes. Who knows, I might even get that elusive pay rise?!'

Remaining calm is a choice that can make a huge difference to how we experience our work–life worlds. You have a choice – would you like to be calm or anxious?

I thought so.

Face the fear and go out and be calm. It's going to make you happier too.

Happiness

Whilst positive thinking tends to amount to a mindset, the quest for happiness is an active intention which can clearly impact on our approach to a work–life balance. If we do things which contribute to happiness, we're going to improve the experiences. However, the manifestation of happiness is open to a raft of different interpretations. What makes me happy might not necessarily make you happy. I feel happy when the Scottish national football team wins a match, which, admittedly, isn't very often. Unless you're Scottish, you might not share my happiness. Surprise, yes, but not necessarily happiness.

Some of us might regard happiness as part of faith or worship within a religion or having compassion and love for others. For others, it might be more humanistic in terms of self-control, self-management and self-actualization. Or there could be a more philosophical construct.

I define happiness broadly as a positive, subjective wellbeing, experienced in the here-and-now. We can't be happy about the future as it hasn't happened yet and we can't control fully what will. Similarly, we might reflect on a happy moment from the past but the actual experience of happiness is felt in the present.

Many cultures and societies have a preoccupation with striving to be happy as if this is a panacea for all. Our definition of happiness can become confused in a pursuit of pleasure. Have a think back to the section in Chapter 4 on page 119 about delayed gratification and you'll start to see a differentiation between pleasure and happiness. A quest for pleasure can become boring or overwhelming; because it is an emotion often experienced in short-term bursts, trying to achieve it can feel relentless. I might treat myself with a single, cold Guinness after a long day hiking through the hills. That could give me a taste-pleasure sensation and a sense of happiness about my achievement. Having six pints of Guinness may enhance the pleasure but would probably undo the happiness due to the likely adverse consequences. There should be a balance to everything.

Creating a successful work–life balance very much taps into the need for a fluid, calibrating mechanism. It's never static because there are so many variables we just don't have control over. Likewise with happiness. Positive, subjective wellbeing may come under fire from difficult and challenging experiences which might thwart, undermine or conspire against happiness.

The irony, to some degree, is these challenging times can increase the intensity, meaning and enjoyment of happier ones. There's an increasing body of evidence to suggest that pain, loss, failure and trauma can generate in us a transformational growth, psychological immunity and resilience.[4]

This is not to say that we should seek out stress or trauma, nor does it diminish the pain and suffering we might feel when experiencing such scenarios. Ultimately, it's about how we interpret and make sense of such events. As we discussed in Chapter 1, purpose and meaning, as a component of work–life balance, can impact our definition and experience of happiness.

Torvin

In his late 50s, Torvin experienced the death of both his parents within a short space of time. This shook his psychological grounding and emotional foundation as he struggled to cope with his loss. After a period of sickness absence from work, he felt he needed to get back into the structure and routine of his publishing job. However, whilst the job had not changed, he had. Soon, he found himself counting the days before he could retire and get his pension. He thought that his job had offered freedom and choice but he now saw it differently as a role determined by his publisher and clients, not him.

The bereavement made him realize he had not been happy before; he just had some illusion of happiness and work–life functionality. The work we did together combined coping with bereavement, understanding how this impacted who he was as a person and his meaning of life. He worked out he could retire at the age of 60, rather than the previously proposed 65, without a significant pension income detriment and we ended with his decision to make a break. The last I heard from him was via a postcard he sent from the Danube in Germany, explaining he had landed a freelance job as a travel writer for river cruises and was happier now that he could ever remember.

My work with Torvin made me realize that our definition and construct of happiness can change in an instant. If we pause to consider what happiness means to us in any given point in our lives, we may realize it is different to what we thought. Conversely, we might find that our lives really are enriched and nourished sufficiently and that unbeknown to us, we are happy. If you're happy and you know it, clap your hands! Give this segment a high score in your work–life balance scoring system in this book and move on to an area that requires attention.

Our work–life balance will shift and change over time in relation to life events. We might be in the same job we were three years ago, but we will have gained three years more life experience and the wisdom that comes with this. Similarly, our construct of happiness might have changed too.

The secret of creating a successful work–life balance is to conduct the scoring system used in this book on a regular basis. One small shift in one segment can have a significant impact on others. All too often, we can sail through life with minimal thought to our work–life balance, content to chug along and settle into the mainstream comfort zone.

If there's one thing I have realized from being a therapist, it's that we fail to take preventative and proactive action before the build-up of stress immobilizes effective functioning.

Needs and wants

As we work to define what happiness means to us, it is worth spending a moment to consider the difference between needs and wants. Needs are largely necessary for our survival or to complete a goal or task. These might include home-based needs such as a roof over our heads or enough money to pay the bills. At work, we need the time and resources to enable us to do our job.

Wants are generally a desire for something which might enrich our lives in some way, but are not necessary. A need for me is a reliable car to get me to work. A want may be that Porsche 911. The latter may enrich my driving experience but won't meet a need any better.

There can be consequences where wants conflict with needs. The Porsche 911 might significantly damage my bank balance to the detriment of needs such as food and bills. We'll cover Money and Finances in the next chapter but suffice it to say here, much stress and conflict occurs in our life, particularly our work–life balance, when the cost of our wants (including the impact of debt) sabotages our needs.

Happiness can emerge simply from a realization that we need less than we think. Not only will this save us money but we'll also learn to better appreciate what we do have. Personally, I would probably find greater satisfaction from owning five good pairs of shoes, rather than a cupboard of 55 mediocre pairs.

I know of a number of people who derive great fun and enjoyment from using auction and community shopping websites to sell what they really don't need and to de-clutter their homes (and lives). One of my neighbours even used to save the inside cardboard from toilet rolls, then sell them en masse via an auction website for craft enthusiasts who needed them for their hobbies.

Choice and control

As I've discussed throughout this chapter, many of us like to feel in control. Much of this involves familiarity, routine, structure and the status quo but life, predictably, has unpredictability written all over it. This ambiguity can present us with things we don't know and this is when we start to strive for control, to bring that familiarity and structure back into place. But it's worth thinking about why we need control. In many cases we don't. It is the perception of control that hooks us. The reality is we need less control than we think. When we release this compunction to control we can experience an enormous freedom.

What can help is having choices and with this we have opportunities. The work–life balance scoring system will illustrate which aspects of our lives need attention and consideration. Choice, however, will determine priorities and outcomes. In this chapter, I may have a comparably low score under 'stress' and 'happiness' so I might choose to attend to the stressors in my life in the hope this will open up a more natural happiness. Alternatively, it might be that choosing to focus on happiness will reduce my feelings of stress.

We can't change something that's happened but we can choose how we think, feel or act in relation to this. Edinburgh, the capital of Scotland, has recently introduced significant speed restrictions on many of its city centre roads to 20 miles per hour. Recently, I attended a conference there and driving away along an unfamiliar stretch, I think I was zapped by a speed camera. I wouldn't have been driving at much above that limit but I still spotted the tell-tale flash in the rear-view mirror. It really annoyed me. What an idiot I was. Why couldn't I have paid greater attention?

During my return journey to Aberdeenshire, I realized I couldn't do anything about a pending fine but I could choose how I felt, thought and acted towards it. I could choose to mutter obscenities under my breath for the whole three-hour return journey, for instance. From a thought point of view, I chose a reality check. If it was me and I had been caught speeding then that would be it. Fact. Lesson learnt. I'd pay the fine and pay closer attention next time. Emotionally, I chose to listen to soothing jazz music and attend to my breathing to calm me down. I was annoyed and frustrated in the immediate aftermath but I didn't need to be now. Behaviourally, I drove back home with the hazard-perception and speed-monitoring skills of a fighter pilot.

Our work–life balance can be peppered with how we react to unexpected events. It's normal, and in some situations even helpful, to respond to these in the heat of the moment but we do have choices to mitigate the impact on us. My example demonstrated that whilst I had no apparent control over what happened, or at least the aftermath of it, the existence of a series of choices did bring back control into my world.

It's worth adding a disclaimer to the choices giving us control. Sometimes we find that certain choices can cause us conflict or stress because they might spar with or oppose each other. In this way, we might need to make some tough decisions. Creating a successful work–life balance is all about making decisions, some more difficult than others; we have to choose what's important to us in the moment or for the future.

It's easy for doubt to emerge. What if we make the wrong choice? What if things will change forever? It's always important, though, to bear in mind that maybe we won't make the wrong choice. Maybe things could change forever, but for the good.

Martin

After being made redundant from the oil and gas industry, Martin spent 18 months unemployed. He and his wife then picked up part-time jobs which were just enough to financially support them and their five-year-old son. Martin was then suddenly head-hunted for a lucrative posting in Azerbaijan. His wife and son didn't want to go, so Martin had to choose: work away for a significant period of time without them, but boost their finances considerably, or stay at home to find other opportunities. Martin choose to forfeit the opportunity and keep things as they were. For him, and his family, their life together was more important than the greater affluence that the separation would bring.

Was Martin's decision the right one? Would you have made the same choice? It doesn't really matter. What was right for Martin and his family at the time was the basis of their decision. Without the benefit of hindsight, we can only make decisions from the information we have at the time. In itself, this will always be our legitimate and reliable defence; we did what we thought was right at the time.

In many cases, the more we drill down the pros and cons behind any competing choices, the more we are likely to find a clear winner.

Mental health and wellbeing

From a work–life balance perspective, our mental health is just as important a wellbeing barometer as our physical health. Both have a significant impact on each other.

In 2018, NHS England invested only about 13 per cent of funding on mental health.[5] Would you say that your mental health commands the same percentage ratio of your time and investment against your physical health? Is this an appropriate balance? Around one in four of us will experience a mental health issue each year.[6] Consider how this might impact immediate family, friends or work colleagues as well as home and work routines.

There's been stigma surrounding mental health conditions, often involving misconceptions around how they manifest in people and how they are treated. There has also been confusion and assumptions made about how to define mental ill-health, as though only some illnesses or experiences 'count'. Some people tell me they don't like the word 'mental' in 'mental health' as it conjures up all sorts of negative connotations (many may find 'psychological' or 'emotional' health to be better alternative terms). All of this can result in some people not recognizing if their mental health is deteriorating or not feeling able to seek help.

If you've ever felt anxious or experienced a low mood, this can still come under the umbrella of mental ill-health. Though it may not be something to be immediately concerned about (as I've mentioned, we will all experience moments of anxiety, stress, and negative thinking in our lives), it's important to acknowledge these experiences should they become more regular or intense. We all need to be honest and open about our mental health, even just with ourselves, so that we can seek support when we need it.

Suicide: help and support

In 2017, nearly 6,000 people died by suicide in the UK. This number excludes the many more who made suicide attempts. It is unclear how many more people this may include. Suicide is the leading cause of death for the 20–34 age group, with three times more men dying than women.[7]

If you have experienced such thoughts, or have been affected by suicide in any way, I encourage you to reach out for support – to friends and family, to your work's employee assistance programme, to a trained therapist or counsellor, or to one of the dedicated services here:

- Samaritans – www.samaritans.org/ phone: 116 123.
- Mind – www.mind.org.uk, phone: 0300 123 3393.
- HopeLineUK – (for people under 35) papyrus-uk.org/hopelineuk/, phone: 0800 068 4141.
- Prevent Suicide App – www.preventsuicideapp.com/index.html.
- Childline – (for people under 19) www.childline.org.uk/, phone 0800 1111.
- Silverline – (for older people) www.thesilverline.org.uk/, phone 0800 4 70 80 90.
- CALM – (for men) www.thecalmzone.net/, phone 0800 58 58 58.
- Breathing Space – (Scotland) breathingspace.scot/, phone 0800 83 85 87.
- Suicide Prevention Helpline (USA) suicidepreventionlifeline.org/, phone 1 800 273 8255.
- Crisis Services Canada – (Canada) www.crisisservicescanada.ca/, phone 1 833 456 4566.
- LifeLine – (Australia) www.lifeline.org.au/, phone 13 11 14.

Mental wellbeing is a dynamic mental state in that it can change over the short and long term. If we're experiencing ups and downs, it can be useful to start tracking this in a mood diary to see if any trends are emerging. Sometimes it can be difficult to decipher what's going on for us until we begin to spot some clues. If we consistently experience a low mood on Sunday evening, maybe this is telling us something about a reluctance to go to work on

Monday? Or anxiety about the weekly lunch with the in-laws might be suggesting we have a difficult relationship with these people. Fluctuations throughout the day may indicate a diet deficiency. There may be a weather or daylight variables. There are many external influences which contribute to our moods and it's important to understand what affects us individually.

The ABCDE model of stress triggers discussed earlier on in this chapter can alert us to signs of deteriorating mental health. How to combat these triggers depends on what they are and is beyond the scope and space of this book. However, there are clusters of things we can do to improve our mental health. The first three are the most important: communicate, communicate and communicate.

It's OK not to feel OK. Talking about how we feel allows us to express ourselves and make a connection with someone else. It really is good to talk. We might not get or want answers, but the power of being able to open up and feel heard by another is huge. Whilst it's important to be able to actively listen to, be available for and empathize with other people, sometimes it is us who need a shot in the driver's seat; maybe we're the ones who need to be listened to and heard.

Check back to the section in Chapter 1 on communication and listening skills. It further resonates with the next tip, which is to look out for and after other people. Asking if someone is OK when you suspect they might not be could save a life. Having this empathic recognition can make all the difference.

At home, we might have children, parents or relatives who just get on with their stuff in their own worlds. Checking in with them allows them to share these worlds and can help to dispel isolation or loneliness. Similarly, our work colleagues might appear fine on the surface but if your intuition is telling you differently, then it's worth sensitively and appropriately asking how they are doing.

Reframing is another powerful mental health improvement tool. It involves reshaping negativity into positivity. It might be semantics but the power of words is underrated. I think my favourite book is a thesaurus. I love to find the precise word that better fits how I feel or to describe an experience. Next time you feel 'nervous', replace it with the word 'excitement'. You'll have exactly the same behavioural symptoms but the interpretation, meaning and outcome can be very different.

Another tool I use is to encourage my clients to schedule spending the next seven days writing down three things they feel grateful for each day. This can be simple things, including getting to work on time, the weather, a 'thank you' or a smile from a work colleague or finishing the report you've just finished. It could also be having a tidy home, eating a tasty meal, cleaning the car or walking the dog.

Why don't you try it?

At the end of the week you'll have 21. Reading back over 21 things you've been grateful for over the last week is a feel-good tonic in itself. A couple of years ago, I got a letter from a former client who had started a one-week 'grateful' endeavour and managed to keep it up for a year. He had stockpiled and chronicled over a thousand things for which he had been grateful. Imagine how that must have felt to reflect on.

A major inhibitor to maintaining our mental wellbeing, and creating an effective work–life balance, is when we fail to give enough space and attention to ourselves. It's not about being totally selfish, but we need to give ourselves space to appreciate, nurture and enjoy who we are as unique and wonderful individuals. This might involve having a long soak in a bath, listening to a favourite track of music, going for a walk or just spending time in the peace and quiet being mindful. At a deeper level, I believe it is true that it is difficult to love another person if we have not first learnt to love ourselves. Love is about connectedness, closeness, appreciation, interest and affection. It might feel a bit weird to love ourselves but that's because few of us try it.

In a similar vein, how do we have fun? What does fun mean to you and when did you last experience it? Having fun, whether alone or with others, makes us feel good, so it's key to do it as much as we can.

Expressing our creativity and learning is a way to keep our minds healthy and functioning. It's when we get into a rut, feel bored or apathetic that we can inadvertently open the door to low mood and negativity. An adaptation of the previous idea is the challenge to either express your creativity in some form, or learn something new that you didn't know before, each day. This can be great fun when adapted to both our work and home lives, especially when doing it with others.

Improving or giving practice to something we're good at helps to reinforce our strengths and helps us enjoy what we know we can do. In fact, ditching the things we're not good at or don't enjoy is important to free us from stress clutter. Again, we have a choice: hang in there for a hard-won achievement or choose something more appropriate and achievable. Remember the MARTYR acronym for achieving goals?

Three further underrated words we do not use enough are 'thanks', 'no' and 'sorry', but all of these can have some impact on maintaining our mental wellbeing. The first allows us to express gratitude and appreciation and reinforce our connection with other people. 'No' gives us permission and a right to assert ourselves appropriately; it's important to not take on too much. Saying 'sorry' introduces the potential for forgiveness from someone else and for enabling us to learn to offer forgiveness.

Mental health and wellbeing affects us all in different ways, and creating a successful work–life balance means attending to this in all aspects of our home and work lives. A gap or shortfall in one is likely to impact the other. Pretty much every section of every chapter of this book has the potential to impact mental health and wellbeing, including the following section on Physical Health and Wellbeing. This section here services to nail its importance further.

Physical health and wellbeing

Whilst mental health and wellbeing is what's going on in our mind, physical health and wellbeing covers the rest of our body, including what goes in and what comes out. There are three broad components which we'll cover: exercise, diet and sleep. These all have a significant relationship to our work–life balance as they will help us muster the energy to meet our daily demands, or not as the case may be.

There is no specific template for physical health and wellbeing as we're unique human beings not machines… yet in some ways we are machines. We have a complex physiology and biology which needs to be managed effectively in order for us to generate the output required. We need to look after this beautiful machine too. If we neglect or abuse it, we'll experience problems or perform below our capacity. The challenge is to learn about and understand how our bodies work and what they need to obtain maximum efficiency. This includes learning how and when we need to relax, recuperate and recharge. We only have one body. Once it's gone, it's gone.

Exercise

The World Health Organization (WHO) recommends that those of us between the ages of 18 and 64 should engage in at least 150 minutes of moderate-intensity aerobic physical activity or 75 minutes of vigorous-intensity aerobic exercise (or equivalent combination) each week.[8] This should be carried out in bouts of at least 10 minutes. Muscle-strengthening exercises, with weights or using the body as weights, should be conducted at least twice per week using repetitions of about 10. The WHO also encourages us to increase this further to derive even greater health benefits.

Before we launch into a dramatic fitness regime on the Olympian spectrum, it's important to assess our limitations and capacities. If we have a medical condition or health risks it would be prudent to meet with an appropriate medical healthcare practitioner to consider our capabilities and make reasonable adjustments.

Exercise and fitness are a crucial part of our work–life balance and so need to be routinely scheduled into our week. Even more importantly, it should be fun. We need to enjoy, look forward to and reap the benefits from it. How we achieve this is up to us.

The chart in Table 5.2 gives us an idea of what constitutes 'moderate-intensity' or 'vigorous-intensity' aerobic exercise. The key is about increasing your heart rate and speeding up the breathing.

Apart from the physical gains, even moderate-intensity exercise can bring about positive mental health benefits, including mental functioning (speed and attention), mood improvement and increasing energy levels.

Several of the examples above give us the opportunity to engage with others and build camaraderie, especially if activities are team-based. Not only does this provide an added, helpful social dimension but we may be more likely to carry through with the activity because we don't like to let people down.

How can you build physical exercise into your routine? We all say we just don't have enough time but more often than not it's about creating the time and being ruthless about this. It might mean adjusting our schedule, but the benefits will outweigh any sacrifices. If you while away the evening hours watching television, what about going to bed a bit earlier, setting your alarm an hour before you're normally awake and start your day with your exercise plan? It could involve a brisk walk, a swim or a bout in the gym. This will help you wake up, you'll feel much more refreshed and your mind will be alert faster.

Table 5.2 Exercise activities

Moderate intensity	Vigorous intensity
Gentle swim	Fast swim
Walking at pace	Jogging or running
Cycling at moderate pace	Cycling fast or up and down hills
Hiking or hill-walking	Football or rugby
Netball or volleyball	Hockey or lacrosse
Household activities like vacuuming or mowing	Aerobics, spin or gymnastics
Dancing or skipping	Tennis
Yoga	Badminton
Pilates or Tai Chi	Squash

Alternatively, we might find that weekends offer the time and space. Perhaps bring family or friends together for a hike in the countryside, a hill walk, a forest cycle?

If you don't currently engage in sufficient exercise, I challenge you to choose an activity which is right for you and schedule this routinely over two weeks. I pretty much guarantee that after this period of time, you'll either ditch the activity for something more preferable or you'll have got the bug and you'll want to sustain the progress. The more we do this, the more we'll experience the many physical and mental health benefits that fitness and exercise can generate.

Nutrition/diet

It's difficult to summarize a comprehensive diet and nutrition guide that's sufficient for the majority of us and our bodily needs, whilst also attending to individual differences and health requirements. For this section, I'll focus on nutrition and diet which can impact our moods and mental health.

As this chapter blends psychological with physical wellbeing, the following guidance for nutrition and diet comes from the UK mental health charity, Mind:

> If your blood sugar drops you might feel tired, irritable and depressed. Eating regularly and choosing foods that release energy slowly will help to keep your sugar levels steady. If you don't drink enough fluid, you may find it difficult to concentrate or think clearly. Vegetables and fruit contain a lot of the minerals, vitamins and fibre we need to keep us physically and mentally healthy.

> Your gut can reflect how you are feeling emotionally. If you're stressed or anxious this can make your gut slow down or speed up. For healthy digestion you need to have plenty of fibre, fluid and exercise regularly. Protein contains amino acids, which make up the chemicals your brain needs to regulate your thoughts and feelings. It also helps keep you feeling fuller for longer.

Caffeine is a stimulant, which gives you a quick burst of energy, but then may make you feel anxious and depressed, disturb your sleep (especially if you have it before bed), or give you withdrawal symptoms if you stop suddenly. Your brain needs fatty acids (such as omega-3 and -6) to keep it working well. So rather than avoiding all fats, it's important to eat the right ones.

SOURCE ©Mind. This information is published in full at www.mind.org.uk

Forbes

When I met Forbes for our first consultation, like with all my clients, I offered him a tea/coffee/water and led him to the kitchen area. I like to enable them to make what they want at the strength that suits. Watching him add in three heaped spoonsful of instant Douwe Egbert coffee with his slightly shaky hands presented me with an immediate observation I stored for any relevant conversation. He presented with stress at work and, slightly unsurprisingly, he spoke of his 10 cups of coffee a day, plus colas, as his way of coping. When we explored whether this was in fact exacerbating his situation he volunteered to reduce his caffeine in a managed way. In combination with several stress-management actions, he returned for a follow-up appointment more cool, calm and collected, albeit still grateful for a coffee.

Sometimes we just need to have a little bit more information about what we're putting into our bodies. I find the *Eatwell Guide* from NHS England (Figure 5.3) is a helpful visual guide.

What we consume will have a significant impact on our energy, mood and cognitive functioning. The more healthily we can feed this human machine of ours, the more able we will be to cope and manage the requirements on us in our home and work lives.

Figure 5.3 The Eatwell Guide

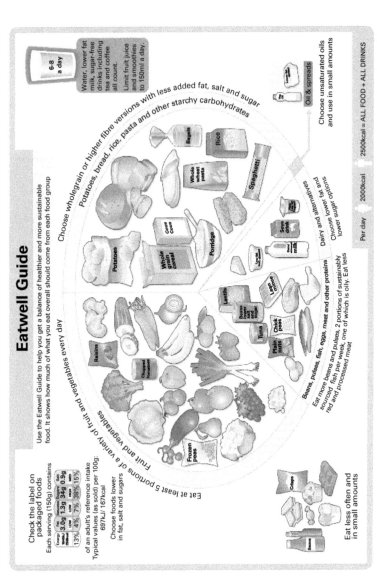

Eatwell Guide

Use the Eatwell Guide to help you get a balance of healthier and more sustainable food. It shows how much of what you eat overall should come from each food group.

Check the label on packaged foods

Each serving (150g) contains

Energy 1046kJ 250kcal	Fat 3.0g	Saturates 1.3g	Sugars 34g	Salt 0.9g
13%	LOW 4%	LOW 7%	HIGH 38%	MED 15%

of an adult's reference intake
Typical values (as sold) per 100g: 697kJ/ 167kcal

Choose foods lower in fat, salt and sugars

Choose wholegrain or higher fibre versions with less added fat, salt and sugar

Potatoes, bread, rice, pasta and other starchy carbohydrates

Bagels

Rice

Whole wheat pasta

Spaghetti

Cous Cous

Potatoes

Whole grain cereal

Porridge

Eat less often and in small amounts

Crisps

Raisins

Chopped tomatoes

Frozen peas

Eat at least 5 portions of a variety of fruit and vegetables every day

Fruit and vegetables

6-8 a day

Water, lower fat milk, sugar-free drinks including tea and coffee all count.

Limit fruit juice and smoothies to 150ml a day.

Oil & spreads

Choose unsaturated oils and use in small amounts

Soya drink

Low fat soft cheese

Plain nuts

Lean mince

Lentils

Beans

Tuna

Chick peas

Dairy and alternatives

Choose lower fat and lower sugar options

Beans, pulses, fish, eggs, meat and other proteins

Eat more beans and pulses, 2 portions of sustainably sourced fish per week, one of which is oily. Eat less red and processed meat

Per day 2000kcal 2500kcal = ALL FOOD + ALL DRINKS

SOURCE Public Health England in association with the Welsh Government, Food Standards Scotland and the Food Standards Agency in Northern Ireland. Reproduced under Crown Copyright 2015/Open Government Licence v3.0.

Sleep

Popular wisdom suggests we need around eight hours sleep a night but some of us function perfectly well on less whilst others need more. Babies and children need more sleep than adults over 60 years old.

Sleep allows our mind and body to rest naturally so we can awaken feeling revived and refreshed. At least, that's the plan. Many of us, however, do have difficulty either keeping to a regular sleep pattern or find that the stresses of the day invade and infiltrate the capacity to sleep peacefully. If we're not asleep within a relatively short space of time, we often start thinking about the fact that we're not sleeping. This generates anxiety, which increases our pulse and heart rate, which keeps us awake further. It can be a vicious cycle. Insomnia can feel like a curse and yet it can give us a clear indication that things are not OK.

Sleep is a functional necessity and part of our physical and mental work–life balance. If we rest well, we'll have the energy to manage our daily lives. If we don't, we'll feel sluggish and lethargic, and may be prone to lower performance, reduced concentration or become more susceptible to accidents and mistakes.

If the sleep strategy tips below don't make a sufficient difference or any sleep blips are not temporary, it might be worth checking with your doctor or medical health practitioner in case you have some underlying medical condition.

Work–life balance action
Sleep strategy

Caffeine	Avoid caffeine in the evening, ideally stopping mid-afternoon
Wind-down	Prepare for bedtime with a step-down reduction of activity and stimulation
Exercise	Keep to a regular daytime exercise regime – see exercise recommendations above
Dinner	Schedule dinner earlier so your body has time to digest before sleep
Alcohol	Avoid alcohol as this can interfere with sleep patterns

Mindfulness	Try a short guided meditation in or before bed to help you relax
Breathing	Adopt the 4/7/8 breathing exercise – inhale for 4 seconds, hold for 7, exhale for 8
Routine	Keep to a regular pattern to maintain sleep cycles
Blue light	Avoid 'blue light' a few hours before bed, ie tablets/iPads, mobile phones, etc
Worries	Suspend any worries by writing them down and parking them until morning
Napping	Resist and avoid daytime napping so you concentrate sleep at night
Environment	Create the appropriate comfort, temperature, darkness and quietness
Wash	Have a bath or shower to relax and cleanse the body and mind
TV	Record and watch early in the evening rather than invading your sleeptime

You'll know from experience that if you have rested well, you'll be so much more 'in the zone' for your job, with sufficient energy to return home at the end of the day and do what you need to do. Some people say they are not good in the mornings to legitimize 'night-owl' tendencies of staying up later. However, I have yet to find any plausible evidence to suggest this cannot be re-jigged so we can adjust to an earlier sleep routine that gives us the rest we deserve.

If you're reading this book as a calm-down, relaxation strategy in bed at night... I hope you sleep well.

'Get a Life' needs audit scaling system: psychological and physical wellbeing

The scaling system in the following table applies for each section discussed in this chapter and is based on your personal perception of whether there is a deficiency, imbalance or need... or not.

Everyone is different so there's no right or wrong. This simply allows you to consider the gaps that exist for you.

The scoring uses a self-rating percentage index from 0–100 with 0 per cent referring to needs totally **unmet** and 100 per cent equating to needs totally **met**. Add up the percentage totals and divide this by the number of sections to give you a total percentage for this chapter. At the end of the book, you will have a percentage total for each chapter, giving you scope to consider where you need to prioritize action.

If any sections are irrelevant to you, ignore them and reduce the number of sections you divide this by accordingly.

	Sections	Percentage of needs currently met %
1	Stress management	
2	Positive thinking	
3	Calmness	
4	Resilience	
5	Happiness	
6	Mental health	
7	Exercise	
8	Diet/nutrition	
9	Sleep	
Total Score for Chapter 5 (out of 900%): Psychological and Physical Wellbeing		
Divide this Total Score by **9**		
Total Percentage Score (out of 100%) for Chapter 5		

For the more visually minded, plot a dot on the radar diagram in Figure 5.4 with the same percentage scale: 0 for needs totally unmet up to 100 per cent for needs totally met. You can then join the dots together to form a needs audit radar. This method gives you a visual cue to identify the gaps in your needs.

Figure 5.4   Psychological and physical wellbeing needs audit radar

This chapter on Psychological and Physical Wellbeing has focused on what makes us a well-oiled, fully functioning human being, integrating the wellness of our body and mind. If we ignore this, we'll have no hope in creating a successful work–life balance. This is a precursor to giving us the framework with which everything else flows and allows us to better manage stress and become more resilient.

The next chapter covers a series of Practical Factors to give you the background tools and optimal environment to maximize your work–life balance. In this final chapter, I'll also conclude the work–life balance scoring system so you can integrate the scores from all preceding chapters. In this summary scoring, you'll get the best picture yet of your current work–life balance, where the gaps exist and where action is required. Then it's up to you.

Endnotes

1 Yerkes, RM and Dodson, JD (1908) The relation of strength of stimulus to rapidity of habit-formation, *Journal of Comparative Neurology and Psychology*, **18** (5), pp 459–82

2 Kabat-Zinn, J (2017) *Be You Fully: Body scan exercise* [Online video]. Available from: www.youtube.com/watch?v=15q-N-_kkrU&feature= youtu.be (archived at https://perma.cc/PAR7-GS83)

3 Nietzsche, F (1889/1968) *Twilight of the Idols,* ed/tr R J Hollingdale, Penguin, New York

4 Tedeschi, RG and Calhoun, LG (1995) *Trauma and Transformation: Growing in the aftermath of suffering,* Sage Publications, Thousand Oaks, CA

5 NHS England (2019) *Mental Health Five Year Forward View Dashboard.* Available at: www.england.nhs.uk/mental-health/ taskforce/imp/mh-dashboard/ (archived at https://perma.cc/4PUH-775T)

6 McManus, S, Meltzer, H, Brugha, TS, Bebbington, PE and Jenkins, R (2009) *Adult Psychiatric Morbidity In England, 2007: Results of a household survey,* The NHS Information Centre for health and social care

7 Mental Health Foundation (2018) *Suicide.* Available at: www. mentalhealth.org.uk/a-to-z/s/suicide (archived at https://perma.cc/ G5M8-623V)

8 World Health Organization (nd) *Physical Activity and Adults.* Available at: www.who.int/dietphysicalactivity/factsheet_adults/en/ (archived at https://perma.cc/VTR8-9TRH)

06
Practical factors

In this chapter, we focus on some of the practical and physical factors of work–life balance which cover being at home, whether for rest and relaxation or some form of work.

Home and physical environment

We all want to make where we live feel like a home but what does that actually mean? It should offer sanctuary and comfort, security and safety, a sense of belonging and being grounded. We get emotionally attached to our home because it can reflect much of our personality and character. It represents a massive part of our work–life balance, as it will often be our 'go-to' place to relax and get a break from the rigours of our working lives.

Readers may be familiar with an ITV show in the UK originating from the late 1980s called *Through the Keyhole*. In this programme, a host would snoop round a celebrity's house as contestants would try to guess the name of the occupant. Memorabilia, pictures, ornaments, furniture and decorations would all build up the profile and personality of the celebrity.

If the TV crew came to your house, how might the host describe it, and what would they understand about you from it? More importantly, what might your home say about your work–life balance?!

I'm not suggesting that your place should always look like a show-home in case a camera crew drops by, but it's important to consider what effect our living spaces have on us. What sort of mood or ambience do they convey? How do they make us feel? Do we seek peace and relaxation, a sense of family and connectedness, or a vibrancy and sleekness of modern living?

Some people do find a sense of order and cleanliness to be important to them. Others like a form of 'controlled chaos'. I've seen this most strikingly in garden sheds and garages where tools and garden equipment are stored. I marvel at those I have seen where everything is in its rightful place, maskings and clasps for tools on the walls, garden tools in a tidy compartment, tool-boxes neatly stacked and tubs of ironmongery shelves in order. Conversely, I've seen others that look like the aftermath of a medieval battle, whose owners spend more time trying to find something than they do using it.

Cleanliness and tidiness is an individual thing. It's not for me to advise you, only to encourage you to reflect on how your attitude and approach impacts on you and in particular the effect on your work–life balance. When you return home after a long day at work, how does cleanliness and order impact you? It might not matter; maybe you're relieved to be back at home, whatever the state it's in.

Whether it's your desk at work or your home, does having order and structure convey or encourage an ordered and structured mind and approach? Some people have an aversion to 'clutter' in their physical surroundings as it makes them feel similarly in their head-space. Would de-cluttering your home improve how you feel about it? There's a tradition to have a 'spring clean' every year, getting rid of things we don't need or that serve no purpose. Why leave it until the spring? Keeping on top of things may take less time if attended to regularly.

What other affordable changes might you value and appreciate? Visual touches and aesthetics can make a big difference to our homes. This might include how it's decorated or our choices of soft furnishing and covers. Wall art and pictures reflect much of what is important to us: stunning landscapes might illustrate our appreciation of the outdoors; modern art might demonstrate our creative side; family portraits might highlight an affinity with our loved ones; posters of rock bands might connect with our love of music or our inner rebel.

Outside, the garden, if we have one, can represent a further extension of our oasis. The time of year might determine what we can do in terms of planting or pruning but there's no end of possibilities to what can be created. Gardens, plants and greenery represent a living, breathing entity to many people's homes.

Living with others

Whilst there are now more people living alone than at any time before, many of us do live with partners, family or friends. We all want our home to be homely to us but when there are others to add into this mix, we're faced with potentially different and conflicting home needs and wants. How many of us have been irked or annoyed by the living behaviours and attitudes of people with whom we live? This is where compromise and negotiation comes into play.

I can hear the echoes across the land of familiar phrases: 'shut the door', 'shoes off in the hallway', 'pick up your clothes', 'those dishes won't wash on their own', 'would someone please replace the toilet roll when it runs out?' and so on. With children, it can be a constant battle of wits, fighting the need for order against the apathy or rebelliousness of youth. Even with partners or housemates, it's unlikely we will share identical living habits. It can affect our sense of comfort and calmness, disrupting routines that we need to orchestrate our home-based work–life balance.

My Aunt

When I was young, I remember my Aunt explaining that in the early stages of her marriage to my Uncle, his approach to home living was abysmal, at least in her eyes. With her traditionally meek and humble demeanour, smiling sweetly over her cup of Earl Grey tea and Walkers shortbread, she reflected on the need to thoroughly re-educate him, explaining the sensible and pragmatic things he didn't seem to take notice of. Milk would go off more quickly if it was not returned to the fridge. Food dropped and left on the floor would attract germs, insects and vermin. Clothes worn every day would tend to stink after a bit. Even in the naivety of youth, I suspected my Aunt's story was not quite as it was and perhaps amounted to some sage guidance for my benefit!

If we feel flustered and frustrated at home then our work–life balance will be affected simply because home will seem like less of a sanctuary than it might otherwise. The key is being able to talk about what's important to us and, crucially, why.

Similarly, even if you're moving to a remote croft on the Isle of Skye off the west coast of Scotland, we'll all have neighbours. Our relationship with them can influence how we feel about our experience of living there. Having noisy or disruptive people next to us may become our reality and it's important to try to resolve it, rather than accept the situation in silence. We may need to adopt the 'softly-softly' approach, or one which is more assertive, and if it remains a concern, to involve the local authority or police. If doing something is not an option (especially for reasons of personal safety) then moving away might be the only realistic decision.

Moving home

Though hopefully not the result of bad neighbours, most of us will move home at some time in our lives, to upgrade, down-size or to re-locate for work. Wherever we go, again it's about ensuring that it offers us the home part of our work–life balance. Some people say you need to live in a place for a year before you know what needs changing in the decoration or garden. Others move in and want to start afresh immediately. What's going to aid your work–life balance most?

Moving home is also concerned with adjusting to a new neighbourhood, where to find reliable tradespeople, finding out about places to shop or for evening entertainment and generally making the necessary connections to allow you to integrate and live.

Without doubt, moving home can be a stressful experience, especially if you're packing up from one, dealing with the removal whilst also fretting about the mortgage deal going through in time for the new place. It might be prudent, if not already planned, to take some time off work before, during and after, so as to give sufficient time and energy for the upheaval. Moving home might be stressful but it can also be a hugely exciting experience and the beginning of a new chapter in our lives.

Be a tourist

Whether we have just moved or have lived in our home for ages, we often limit our free time to our immediate surroundings. As part of building our life experiences and enriching the home part of our work–life balance, it can be great fun to 'be a tourist' and get to know the area.

When I lived in Edinburgh city centre, I would find myself popular with friends and family who saw an opportunity for free accommodation whilst visiting the place for business or pleasure. It was always lovely to host and socialize but I became aware that many of these visitors would see more of my city than I did. This encouraged me to get out more and savour the sights and sounds of this wonderful place that I called home. Ironically, I found out so much more with a 'tourist' approach than simply living there.

Getting to know our locality or environment helps to widen the essence of what it feels like to live in our home. Our property is just a dot on the map compared to everything the area has to offer, so exploring can improve our connectedness to where we live. Living in rural Aberdeenshire in Scotland, I have on my doorstep the majestic Cairngorm mountain range on one side, quaint fishing villages to the coast, some 300 castles and gardens dotted about the landscape, along with the plethora of Speyside whisky distilleries. I'm still trying to experience them all (in moderation, of course).

Working from home

Many organizations are aware of the importance of maintaining a work–life balance, and offer a range of flexible working arrangements to support this, including working from home. They appreciate this can work to our advantage and take the commute out of the equation. From a work–life balance perspective this can make a huge difference, particularly if we travel long distances, have impacting health conditions or juggle carer's responsibilities. The first time I worked for an organization from home, I kept the same 9–5 working day but at 5pm I would head out for a 45-minute walk, which was the exact time I'd otherwise be returning home in the car.

Organizations might benefit by reducing the office space they require, saving wear and tear on furniture and equipment, reducing utility costs and overall lowering their carbon footprint, so it can be a win–win scenario.

It can feel like an alluring prospect to ditch the formal demeanour of the workplace for the more relaxed environment of home but it's not always quite so easy. It needs planning, focus and organization, plus appropriate privacy, resources and space.

Andy

With his job in IT architecture, Andy only really needed his computer to do his work so when he got a chance to work from home he leapt at the opportunity. The experience was not quite as he expected. Hemmed into a restrictive, tiny office space, there seemed to be a constant drone outside of a neighbour's leaf blower or lawnmower, his sister and her toddlers would pop by unannounced on a regular basis and his dog seem to bark at everything from spiders to the neighbour's cat. Rather than offering him an improved work–life balance it created a conflict between the two. He was back in the office within a month. Andy needed the focused, dedicated and quiet atmosphere of his workplace to give him the physical and noise-controlled environment to concentrate and be effective. Rather than offering him an improved work–life balance it created a conflict between the two.

An additional frustration which can be experienced working from home is a sense of isolation both from our work colleagues and from wider social circles. It makes us realize that social interaction forms an important part of our experience of life at work; even phone calls and video conferencing don't quite match the impact of working in the same physical space. We might sometimes feel a bit forgotten, whether in official updates or just for informal gatherings; as the saying goes, 'out of sight, out of mind'. Working from home may require us to make an increased effort to connect with others beyond what we might require if in the office.

In an office environment, it may be easier to remember to take sufficient breaks from our desks and computer screens. These breaks can include getting a drink to stay hydrated (though water-based, coffee and tea are poor replacements for water), or simply stretching our legs after a period of sitting down. Whatever the reason, taking brief breaks helps to sustain concentration and focus.

The other side of this may be that when working from home, it is easier to become distracted because there's no one to check in with us, or to motivate us. We may find ourselves having more frequent drink or snack breaks than necessary, getting on with the housework, zoning out on social media, watching daytime TV or, as Finn found, getting caught out.

Finn

I worked with sun-loving Finn in a career-coaching capacity at a time when he was somewhat bored in his job. When we first met, he explained to me that a device on his computer had a facility for his organization to monitor his activity – something his team of home-working colleagues all had. If he tapped something on his keyboard or moved his mouse, his activity monitor would show green. After 15 minutes of inactivity it would turn red. He proudly revealed he had found a way to aid the 'life' bit of his work–life balance by running an electrical extension cable outside to power his laptop and dangle his mouse over the arm of his sun-lounger, zapping the mouse at periodic intervals whilst he relaxed in the sunshine.

He got away with this until one day he remembered at the last minute that he had a video-conference with board members of a client organization. He quickly put a shirt and tie on for the occasion (aware that's all his viewers would see) and cranked up his laptop from his home office. During the call, he was asked for some statistics. He realized the document he needed was in the filing cabinet behind him, so he went to retrieve them, forgetting that he was wearing straggly shorts until he heard the laughter at the other end of the computer. This got back to his boss and his knuckles were duly rapped.

Whilst some of us may have the opportunity to work from home as part of flexible working, this won't apply for everyone. The one aspect of work–life balance that may affect all of us is the temptation to bring work home. It's your call as to whether you do, and if so how much, but remember the importance of your leisure time for your work–life balance.

Running your own business

Whether you are setting up from your garage or within fancy new premises, starting a business can be a hugely time-consuming and demanding enterprise. There's all the official stuff, such as registering with tax authorities, dealing with banks and insurance companies, managing your accounts, and that's all alongside determining your product or service and seeking out your customers.

If you are starting up from scratch, chances are you'll have been working for someone else before, and will have some significant questions to consider. Do you have savings in place? Is it the right time to make the leap? Do you understand your customers enough? Is your product or service sufficiently viable? Lots of questions. Lots of potential stress. But get it right and it can be a hugely rewarding experience.

In the early 2000s, I was in the lucky position to have bought a small rental property just as the market took off and I sold it within a couple of years, banking a profit, after taxes and fees, of about £20,000. I had had this idea for ages about creating an online, activity-based, social networking business. The idea would be to have enthusiastic champions for up to 50 key sporting, hobby and outdoor activities; they would build up their communities and use the online forum to encourage engagement, create communities and facilitate events in locations around the UK. My budget was £20,000, including what I needed to live on, paying bills, food and so on. I worked on this for 12 hours a day, pretty much seven days a week for a year. It sort of worked and created a lively community for a number of the activities, but not nearly enough to sustain it financially. I'd reached my investment limit so, to avoid getting into debt on limited evidence that the venture would work, I bowed out and closed the business. Sceptics had warned me this sort of online, social networking enterprise would never succeed.

Several months later in early 2004, I got the shock of my life when Facebook launched. It was very similar to my concept in terms of functionality and focus. Hey ho. You win some, you lose some. I had been small fry and perhaps I should have considered seeking outside investment.

Irrespective of whether this could or should have worked, my work–life balance had been horrendous and unsustainable. Sadly though, this is not unfamiliar for many people starting up their own business as the demands on an entrepreneur might skew the balance. It becomes a lifestyle choice and often feels much more personal: you're the boss and success or failure might seem down to you. There's not just the financial investment but your own blood, sweat and tears of time and hard graft. You don't get sick or holiday pay and no employer contributions to a pension plan. The same applies if you run a family business which might have traded for generations. If things work out well, you reap the rewards. But if they don't, you have to suffer the consequences. Such intense involvement can be detrimental to work–life balance.

If you run a small business, where does work–life balance fit in for you? Perhaps you launched it to create a more successful work–life balance because it didn't exist before? Has this become a reality?

Running your own business does mean being your own boss, so in theory you have a potential to determine, map out and schedule your own work–life balance. You still need to look after yourself. Your health and wellbeing remains as important as if you were working elsewhere for someone else.

Janine

After receiving an inheritance investment, Janine decided to buy commercial premises on the outskirts of a busy town and set up a holistic therapy enterprise. She rented rooms to counsellors, chiropodists, osteopaths, massage therapists, acupuncture practitioners and herbalists. Initially she operated as a coach but after reflecting on her own work–life balance, she realized she wanted to be more involved in managing the therapy enterprise and promoting its practitioners. When she heard that her massage therapist was a qualified Tai Chi instructor, an idea formed. From 8.00 to 8.45 every morning she cleared the boardroom and offered free Tai Chi to all her practitioners. Whilst this gave Janine some important 'me time' as part of her work–life balance, it also had the unintended benefit of bonding together the practitioners, most of whom operated in their isolated silos. It has proved so popular that, as far as I know, it still operates today.

A small investment from Janine paid off in her own wellbeing and helped others at the same time. She also found a way to gel together her rent-paying practitioners and create a community where one didn't exist; when you're working alone or for yourself, life can be quite isolating.

Money and finances

We can't get away from the fact that we need money, in some form or another, to survive. The vast majority of us achieve this by working to earn an income. We achieve financial stability if we earn more than we spend. Problems emerge when more goes out than comes in and we start to struggle to make our finances balance. Money issues can be a huge source of stress. It can begin to sabotage our work–life balance, especially if we feel compelled to take on additional jobs to make ends meet or we just spiral into debt. Once in debt, we get caught by the interest trap, which heaps on premiums to repayments and takes us longer to settle.

If you are in debt or teetering on the edge of it, please do check out the Resources section in the Appendix which will offer you some sources of independent advice, help and guidance. I'm not a debt management specialist so will bow out here to those who have such skills.

Have another read of the section in the previous chapter on Needs and Wants and it becomes apparent that we do often struggle to ascertain the difference. Most of us need much less than we think. We might find ourselves in awe, gawping in our local electrical retailer at the 10-foot, ceiling-mounted home cinema projection system, but perhaps a 45-inch TV would be totally sufficient and save us a thousand pounds in the process. The beast of a machine might enhance the televisual experience but if it's at the cost of something else we really do need or we get locked in a high-interest repayment plan, where's the fun in that?

Financial intelligence is a term I use to prompt the personal money management with which we all have responsibility. It's our choice whether we use credit finance in the form of credit cards. Credit cards can offer payment protection in some situations if something goes wrong with the purchase of your product or service. Check with your credit card company to understand what they offer and how, as there can be limitations, terms and conditions. If you do use credit cards ensure you pay off your balance in full each month, so you don't get stung by interest charges. If you can't afford something, don't buy it.

Few of us actually know or understand our financial fluidity at any one time, meaning we're not quite sure what money we have in our bank account until we get our statement or are paid.

Paola

When I met Paola, she presented with stress at work and low mood. When we peeled the onion layers back further, we discovered she spent most evenings out with friends as a way to cope with the job she told me she disliked. This frustration centred on how she felt she was underpaid, and therefore undervalued. Much of her disposable income was spent on socializing, which then exacerbated her financial concerns. I set her a challenge to suspend socializing for two weeks and instead keep in touch with friends and family by phone (she had unlimited free minutes on her mobile phone). When she returned a month later to see me, she reflected on how much money she had saved during those weeks. She proposed significantly reducing her socializing to weekends and one mid-week point and believed she could still save money each month. Paola realized that it was actually her own personal finance management that had caused her concerns; she was paid enough for what she did, and she did like her job. With her refreshed perspective, she now had choices.

Whether we regularly monitor our monthly outgoings or not, the tax point at the end of the financial year gives us a much bigger picture.

A simple but effective way to keep track of our finances is to get into the habit of completing a monthly budget planner. There are some excellent free online versions available and links to these are included in the Appendix.

An example of a monthly budget planner can be found in Table 6.1.

Work–life balance action
Budget planner

The simple budget planner in Table 6.1 gives you a quick summary but might not include all your income and outgoings. Consider extending this to suit your own situation and requirements.

Table 6.1   Monthly budget planner

Month:	Income	Expenditure	Balance
Income			
Mortgage/rent			
Insurance			
Council tax			
Loan repayments			
Gas/electricity			
Phone, TV, broadband			
Car insurance			
Car fuel			
Car repairs			
Groceries/food			
Alcohol/coffee			
Eating out/ socializing			
Clothing			
Family costs			
Home repairs			
Holidays			
Christmas fund			
Medical/dental			
Miscellaneous			
	Total: £	Total: £	
	This: £	**Minus this: £**	**Leaves you: £**

For specific advice and guidance, please consider meeting an independent financial advisor who will be better placed to consider your particular financial situation. The same would apply if you need to get mortgage and pensions advice.

Whilst this section encourages financial prudence and due diligence, including saving where you can, as part of work–life balance, it's important to have a life. I've known people who have become obsessed with saving at the cost of getting out there and enjoying life. It's about getting the right balance: save what you can when you can, but also use your hard-earned income to good effect and enjoy the fruits of your labours.

Information technology and communications

We live in an IT and communications era that has, even just over the last 20 years, transformed how we live our lives. This has proliferated choices and options, giving us the potential to decide what we use and how we engage with those impacting on our lives. It has, of course, also presented us with a new set of difficulties, challenges and problems.

Information technology (IT)

What on earth would we do without computers and smartphones? Few office jobs don't involve some form of IT. Even at home, many of us may have computers or tablets. Thanks to this technology, numerous tasks have become easier and quicker to manage. The internet gives us a potential answer to any question (though in my opinion, nothing can quite beat looking up a word in a paper dictionary or having a discussion with someone via the spoken word). Our greatest challenges seem to be keeping up sufficient IT skills and savviness to operate the machines, whilst managing the angst when the things crash or fail to do what they're supposed to do.

When everything works, modern-day IT can aid our work–life balance by enabling us to work more efficiently; we can get more done in less time. This brings with it an expectation of delivery, and as we rely so much on IT, when things don't work out, our world feels like it is caving in. We need to build in some leverage for IT malfunction, slow-down or crash, so we don't blow a proverbial gasket.

Organizations can sometimes imply that through IT resources, we are available 24/7. It's important to remember, though, that our computers have three key functions on the HOME key: 'sleep', 'shut-down' and 'restart'. These seem to offer a parallel invitation to our work–life balance. There's a time and a place to 'restart' the day, preferably after we have had a decent 'sleep' preceded by a full work 'shut-down'. But do we always manage this?

When we're at work, there may be an IT department to provide and maintain the tools and equipment to do our jobs. At home it's a different matter; it's just us and maybe some internet protection prophylactic. It's usually when we have just spent some inordinate amount of time on a detailed home-based assignment that our computer decides to crash. This might lead us to berate ourselves for not having instigated a back-up for a year, and we may shout at the computer, promising to do it daily in future if only it could please start working again.

Even when our computer does work, we can be driven to distraction by an aging, slow processing speed. As part of my work–life balance, I seem to be getting up in the morning earlier and earlier as I schedule a swim or a work-out at the local gym. My personal computer seems to be diametrically opposed to me as it takes longer and longer to wake up. It's behaving like a rebellious teenager. After pressing the 'on' button, I can now take out the garbage, vacuum the house and still walk the dog before my PC is ready for me. Maybe it's actually a very clever device that's inadvertently encouraging and fostering my enhanced work–life balance. My lesson here: buy the equipment you're able to that will do the job that's required.

Many workplaces will attend to the ergonomics of our computer workstations, with sufficient and comfortable seating, restrictions from dazzling light and a desk that's fit for purpose. By contrast, our home IT spaces might be limited to the kitchen table, sitting on hard wooden chairs and twitching a mouse that gets jammed by toast crumbs from the morning's breakfast. Our workspace needs to be right for us or we'll get fatigue or frustration or both.

There's an increasing tendency in organizations to reduce paperwork by giving everyone laptops for meetings. This is great for the planet but not so good for connection and communication. Nowadays, the period of time before meetings begin is characterized by silence as everyone reads minutes of previous meetings, checks e-mails or looks up relevant information to present. What about speaking to the person next to you, ask how they are, check what they're doing at the moment or what they're up to at the weekend? Engage and connect. Be human.

IT has the great potential to aid our work–life balance but just like a car only works with a driver, we need to take control over how we use and engage with it. As mentioned at the start of this section, a point of consideration is also about how much we choose to rely on IT. The more we put our trust and faith in it, the more it affects us when something goes wrong.

Communications

We connect with different people in different ways depending on a communication mechanism that fits us, the needs of the moment and our lifestyle. I communicate with my 17-year-old nephew through an instant-messaging medium, my 50-year-old sister by mobile phone (it's often a shortish call), my 80-year-old mother by landline telephone (it's often a long call), and pretty much everyone at work via e-mail. Once in a blue moon I might even write someone a letter, but my predominant means of writing via a keyboard or keypad means that I can't decipher my writing any more. I write Christmas, birthday or sympathy cards with the skills (and the speed) of a beginner calligrapher.

Mic

Presenting with work-related stress, Mic explained that he had frosty relationships with his work colleagues. They seemed to be wary of him and treated him with suspicion and caution. We tried to work out what was going on in these relationships by role-playing past conversations. Nothing emerged from this. And then when e-mailing me to postpone our next meeting, I was aware of the curtness and dominant style of his e-mail. When we met again, I asked about his e-mail 'style'. What emerged was how he regarded e-mail as a quick way to communicate the bare facts; nothing more, nothing less. That meant there was no personality in his style and what he communicated did appear demanding and autocratic. I could see how some people might misinterpret and take some offence from this. We worked on adapting a more conciliatory and collaborative style and Mic realized he could do this without too much difficulty. In time, he found his wider communication style mellowed. He understood that his curt e-mail style had morphed into how he spoke at work. Changing something as small as his e-mail communication style softened and improved his relationships.

When starting any new job or with a new team, it can really help to explain our e-mail style to those you're likely to contact frequently. Some people even take offence if we don't start with a salutation such as 'Hi Rick' (as an example). As with verbal communication, discussed in Chapter 1, so much of the way our messages are received is determined not by what we say but how we say it.

Most of us have, at some stage, fired off an e-mail in the heat of the moment and come to regret it. Unfortunately, there doesn't yet seem to be a facility to make a sent e-mail disappear, and even a 'recall' option tends to have the opposite effect and generate greater intrigue and scrutiny over what's being recalled.

The lesson is to think before we send. Once it's gone, it's gone. We don't know what's going to be going on with the recipient when they receive our communication. Maybe they're in a stressed state or perhaps they have some problem at home. We can't control how a recipient might feel but we can take greater responsibility for how and what we e-mail.

As mentioned in the Time Management section of Chapter 4, we often have an expectation that e-mail and text messages should be replied to immediately. The message alert pings on our phone or PC and our immediate curiosity is aroused. Yet, if we all responded immediately to every message we received, we'd never get anything done. There would be a hurricane of distraction. It is also likely to have a seriously damaging effect on our work–life balance.

There's nothing so distracting or annoying as having a conversation with someone who, when they get a message alert, chooses to stop their engagement with us and check their message. The unknown message might stay in the forefront of our mind – who is it, what do they want – but why not suspend the need to act until the time is right? Perhaps we can switch off the alert, display a bit of self-control and choose when it suits us to 'check for messages'.

If you take on board and apply only one source of guidance in this book to create a successful work–life balance, allocate periods of time when you can switch off your e-mail and text alert. It might change your life. Why not give it a go?

Social media management

As a source of information and communication, social media can offer us a wonderful bouquet of platforms through which we can connect and engage with others, be it discussing current news items or sharing our personal experiences. In the olden days, we would live our lives doing what we normally do, then connect with others face-to-face socially or chat on the phone and share our experiences. Now we get to see people's experiences instantly without the need to ask, enquire or even meet up. Ironically, as a mechanism of communication, it can limit and reduce the desire for physical contact with others. Why do we need to communicate when we know what others are doing and can 'react' and ask questions about it immediately?

These 'reaction' options of likes, emojis or short messages form subsidiary communication responses that create a strange expectation that what we communicate on these platforms needs to be worthy of a response. Though why there seem to be so many photographs of food on social media, I'll never really know. One of my friends has recently posted a photograph of their particularly hairy toe, highlighting the need for the nail to be trimmed; next time I see them, I'm going to thank them for that image. Is this the extent of social media's contribution to the world?

Often, if we don't get some positive affirmation, we feel anxious or disappointed. I've even seen indignant and horrified posts from people on some social media platforms when birthdays have not been acknowledged sufficiently. We've become needy to and reliant on the psychological strokes which the social media contact affirmation offers. There's also the FOMO effect, otherwise known as 'fear of missing out'. If we're not involved, then we get anxious that we might miss out on an important engagement, interaction or conversation.

Even when we do achieve contact, responses and affirmations, social media can start to rule and intrude into our lives, sabotaging any attempt at a positive work–life balance. I can think of a number of times I have seen a couple or family on a meal out and everyone's tapping away into their smartphones, nodding and smiling at the engagement with others who are not present yet totally ignoring those who are. What's the point going out socially with anyone any more if we're always going to be elsewhere?

Be present, in the moment, mindful and open to the experience of the here and now.

Emily

Presenting to me with low mood, it became evident that Emily was significantly affected by her social media world. Everyone else seemed to be having more fun and engaged with more friends than her. Additionally, she was starting to measure and monitor herself in terms of how she looked and dressed. All of this was creating unrealistic expectations of and for her. With gentle challenging, she started to see the prefabricated, embellished lives that everyone liked to present on social media and that for everyone, reality was quite different. She came to distance herself from the fakeness and started to enjoy the realness of her world.

In work–life balance terms, the 'life' bit of work–life balance also requires us to be circumspect and judicious about how we use our 'free' time, so we should moderate not just the amount of social media we engage with but also when. If we're spending every leisure moment engaged with social media then we're not really living our lives and having enriched experiences. The blue light we get from smartphones and tablets can also impact on our capacity to sleep, so late-night 'chat' can inhibit the rest we get.

More seriously, there has been a rise in cyber-bullying which can have a devastating impact on its victims. The widespread public nature of such abuse and the number of people who might read vindictive and spiteful comments makes it feel much more visible. We all have responsibility for what we say and how we say it, and this applies to social media as much as to any other form of communication. Careers have been decimated by ill-thought postings, as well as deliberately vindictive ones. Hate crimes and the prosecutions which go with them are on the increase. Even more sadly, suicides have been attributed to the impact of cyber-bulling and social media abuse.

That being said, social media offers means to talk and connect with people across the world instantly, building communities and friendships over shared interests in ways never before experienced. Families separated by long distances can keep in touch more regularly. We might send supportive, encouraging and friendly messages and watch how we can be met with the same positivity in return. We are able to learn more about the experiences of others, open up new opportunities and choices for our own lives... and create that balance to work and life.

A challenge for the consumption of all social media is to engage with it in a way which is necessary and sufficient, rather than a feeder of distraction and procrastination. Social and entertainment aspects of various platforms can tantalize and titillate. Other more work-related networking sites encourage us to share and post items we believe will be of interest to our business community. Whilst this becomes a potential rich resource, do we get the time to fully digest the depth and breadth of material?

Some of us sign up to social media platforms for a specific purpose: to participate in certain discussions, or to grow our business. Many will have jumped into a new media with the enthusiasm of an excited puppy but it takes dedication and motivation to post regularly and build an engaged community. It's true though that some do find 'the way' and clasp the media opportunities, using it to great personal and professional effect. Bloggers are particularly successful in speaking to their distinctive communities, often bridging the gap between brands and consumers, or giving a voice to those who might otherwise remain silent, unappreciated or unheard.

It may well be that social media is responsible for reducing the physical one-to-one contacts we make and enjoy with others but it simply becomes a new, additional means by which we communicate and connect with one another. It's about how we use it to improve the quality of our lives and the relationships we nurture and develop. As we discussed earlier in this book about self-control and gratification delay, prudent and considered management of what we consume can allow us to enjoy and reap the benefits from the correct dosage for us, and this is as true of social media as it is of anything else.

Get it right and it can seriously benefit our work–life balance. We may use it as a source of information, fascination and inspiration. It can help us relax, recover and recuperate. It can make us laugh and cry. It can give us the capacity to forge meaning and purpose. It can encourage us to develop a passion and belief for causes and campaigns. It may help us to learn and enhance our wisdom. It can develop our work skills and capabilities and offer a springboard to career enhancement and development. It can offer us support, companionship and sanctuary when we are in need. It can be, as one of my clients once referred to it as, 'our friend'.

This chapter on Practical Factors has focused on some of the final, functional aspects which will impact our work–life balance. How we make our home our home, and what we do with and in it will have a significant role to play in the balance we create in our lives. Whilst for most of us, our home is separate to and independent from our work lives, for others it will merge together through home or remote working or small business enterprise.

Money management and financial budgeting gives us the clout to choose how we spend our hard-earned income. It's not always easy and it doesn't always balance in the right way, but it will become a chief determinant over the choices we can make to create a successful work–life balance. As long as we can balance our books and meet our necessary and critical financial needs, a successful work–life balance doesn't necessarily have to be led by money. Some of the best things in life are free – love, laughter, friendships, family, happiness, memories, experiences, a smile, connections and so on.

Some other things in life are not free, such as your information technology and communication devices, but they are generally affordable and can contribute to potentially improving and enhancing how we live our lives. The same goes with social media; it can be a source for good or the world's greatest procrastinator.

Work–life balance remains a journey of choices. It is not the place of this book to tell you what to do, rather the purpose is to empower you to consider your options and, armed with as much insight and information as you can muster, make the best decision for you and your situation. As we close off this chapter, the scoring system used throughout this book seeks to help you assess your own evaluation of Practical Factors, where gaps exist and where you may find opportunities to take action and effect change. In the final, shorter, summary chapter, we'll bring together all the scores for each chapter and get the best possible picture of your work–life balance health.

'Get a Life' needs audit scaling system: practical factors

The scaling system in the following table applies for each section discussed in this chapter and is based on your personal perception of whether there is a deficiency, imbalance or need… or not. Everyone is different so there's no right or wrong. This simply allows you to consider the gaps that exist for you.

The scoring uses a self-rating percentage index from 0–100 with 0 per cent referring to needs totally **unmet** and 100 per cent equating to needs totally **met**. Add up the percentage totals and divide this by the number of sections to give you a total percentage for this chapter. At the end of the book, you will have a percentage total for each chapter, giving you scope to consider where you need to prioritize action.

If any sections are irrelevant to you, ignore them and reduce the number of sections you divide this by accordingly.

For the more visually minded, plot a dot on the radar diagram in Figure 6.1 with the same percentage scale: 0 for needs totally unmet up to 100 per cent for needs totally met. You can then join the dots together to form a needs audit radar. This method gives you a visual cue to identify the gaps in your needs.

	Sections	Percentage of needs currently met %
1	Home environment	
2	Working from home	
3	Running your own business	
4	Money and finances	
5	IT and communications	
6	Social media management	
Total Score for Chapter 6 (out of 600%): Practical factors		
Divide this Total Score by **6**		
Total Percentage Score (out of 100%) for Chapter 6		

Figure 6.1   Practical factors needs audit radar

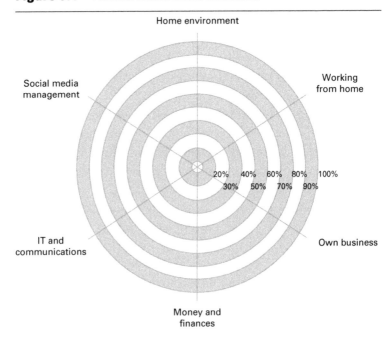

07
Pulling it all together

In the preceding six chapters we have nibbled at a smorgasbord of ingredients which feed into our work–life balance fiesta. Each chapter has focused on a particular segment of the pie, and now we pull these all together to consider the big picture.

Summary of chapters

Creating a successful work–life balance requires us to consider the options, evaluate priorities and needs, then make decisions and choices about how we want or need to live our lives. A work–life balance is a fluid affair; things are moving all the time. The sheer number of influences are banging against each other like atoms; some in a good way but others may generate conflict. There will be times when we feel we have limited options over issues beyond our control.

Yet we do have some capacity to be able to control how we think, feel or act. It is then that we need to manage the issues or shift over to areas for which we can take responsibility. Few things stay static for long and the one constant we can rely on is that change happens all the time. We need to work with it rather than against it.

If you have worked through this book chronologically, rating yourself as you went along, you'll now have the opportunity to plot your scores from the end of each chapter. Here you can start to see where your work–life balance is flowing naturally, or where gaps are starting to emerge.

Scoring your work–life balance

We have covered the following themes:

- Personal development
- People
- Professional issues
- Productivity and performance
- Psychological and physical wellbeing
- Practical factors

Look back to each chapter and add in your percentage scores to the spaces provided below. Then add these together to give a total score in the following table:

Chapter	Topic	Percentage score (%)
1	Personal development	
2	People	
3	Professional issues	
4	Productivity and performance	
5	Psychological and physical wellbeing	
6	Practical factors	
Total Score		

You can also use the scores to map out your overall work–life balance needs audit radar. This will present you with a visual reference and allow you to identify themes and trends (Figure 7.1).

(If you want to see all of your scores together in the same place, the scoring sheets and needs audit radar are available to download for free from the *Get a Life!* book page on the Kogan Page website which accompanies this book).

Figure 7.1 Pulling it all together needs audit radar

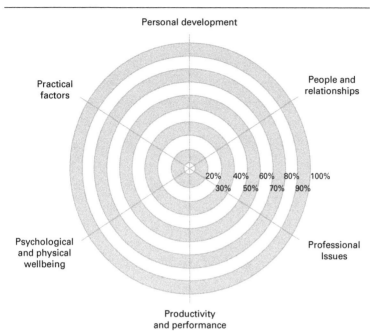

You will be able to see from the above where you have higher and lower scores and your total score represents your overall work–life balance rating as it is today. Then ask yourself:

- Were these the results you expected or do any of them surprise you?
- What do the high scores tell you about how you are meeting your work–life balance needs?
- Can you immediately identify any reasons for the lower scores?

With both of these tools, it's important to remember that there is no right or wrong score. It is impossible that any of us can or would find that our work–life balance is perfect. That's why this is such a challenge and where we all have an opportunity to make necessary changes.

Making your work–life balance

When you have considered these scores, the next step will be to think about how to best make these changes:

- Will you focus on areas with the lowest scores first, or on aspects of your work–life balance that will be easier to improve than others?
- How can you maintain work–life balance successes, rather than allowing them to slip?
- Are there any potential conflicts or obstacles that may impact on improving or maintaining these scores?

Summary of chapter sections

Whilst chapter themes have been developed to best group the various segments and issues discussed within them, you may find that you can better find opportunities to improve by drilling down into more specific sectors. For this reason, I have developed a further unique instrument for you to use.

I've made reference to a couple of UK television gameshows: *Blockbusters* and *Through the Keyhole*. For my third and final inspiration, I'll refer to another hugely popular one – *Wheel of Fortune*, originally hosted by Merv Griffin on the US networks in 1975 with a UK version hitting the screens in 1988. Contestants would spin a huge wheel, and win prizes based on the monetary figures or points the arrow pointed to when it came to a stop.

I've adapted this for a work–life balance purpose. Rather than calling this our wheel of fortune, I think it is much more apt to present this as your Wheel of Future.

The Wheel of Future (Figure 7.2) comprises the key sections from all six chapters of this book, which are also listed below.

Look at all these segments and consider the specific aspects of your work–life balance that you feel require attention. If you don't know where to make a start, visit the Kogan Page website and you'll find an interactive model where you can 'spin the wheel' and randomly stop at a category.

Choose one or two to begin with and think about the following questions:

- What was your initial score for this section?

- Can you identify any specific reasons or influences for this score?

- Do you have an 'end goal' for improving and maintaining this aspect of your work–life balance?

- What decisions or actions do you need to take to achieve this?

Figure 7.2 Work–life balance Wheel of Future

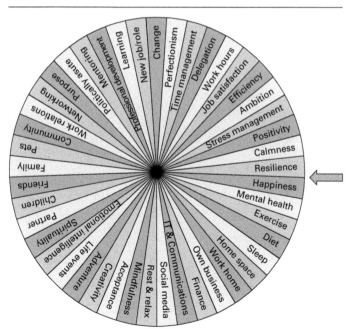

1. *Personal development*

   Rest and relaxation
   Living in the moment
   Accepting situations
   Personal creativity
   Adventure and excitement
   Manage life events
   Emotional intelligence
   Spirituality, faith and religion

2. *People and relationships*

   Partner
   Children
   Friends
   Family
   Pets
   Community
   Work relationships
   Networking

3. *Professional issues*

   Purpose and meaning at work
   Politically astute
   Mentoring and guidance
   Professional development
   Knowledge and learning
   New role or job
   Coping with change
   Perfectionism

4. *Productivity and performance*

   Time management
   Delegation
   Working hours
   Job satisfaction
   Personal efficiency
   Managing ambition

5. *Psychological and physical wellbeing*

   Stress management
   Positive thinking
   Calmness
   Resilience
   Happiness
   Mental health
   Exercise
   Diet/nutrition
   Sleep

6. *Practical factors*

   Home environment
   Working at/from home
   Own business
   Money and finances
   IT and communications
   Social media management

Improving your work–life balance

Your work–life balance is the wheel of your future. It will change all the time and the degree to which you regard it as being successful will be determined by how this evolves, develops and improves in the future.

Return to these tools and scoring systems regularly: every month, quarterly or at whatever interval suits you best. Assess whether the changes you've made have been successful. Identify any new or continued areas for improvement. Celebrate any achievements or new opportunities that you've taken.

Wherever or however you start on your journey to creating a successful work–life balance, please comfort yourself with the understanding that by reading this... you have already started.

APPENDIX
Resources

Much of what has been written revolves around making choices about how we use our time to juggle the demands in our work and life. If we struggle on our own, it can be good to talk to someone. In some cases, we might benefit from or feel the need to reach out to sources of information and support.

The following resources may be of help to you.

> **NOTE:** The following resources are provided in good faith and for information purposes only. They do not constitute endorsement or approval from the author or publisher. You are advised to research and consider your own requirements in order to identify the resources which best meet your needs. No responsibility whatsoever will be accepted for accessing any of the following sources or links nor for any consequences of so doing.

Crisis support

It's OK not to feel OK. If you are struggling or find yourself in a crisis situation, please reach out for support – to friends and family, to your organization's employee assistance programme, to a trained therapist or counsellor, or to one of the dedicated services here:

- Emergency Services UK – 999
- Emergency Services USA and Canada – 911
- Emergency Services Australia – 000

- Samaritans UK – www.samaritans.org/ tel: 116 123
- Samaritans USA – www.samaritansusa.org, tel: 1 (800) 273-TALK
- Mind – www.mind.org.uk, tel: 0300 123 3393
- HopeLineUK – (for people under 35) papyrus-uk.org/hopelineuk/ tel: 0800 068 4141
- Prevent Suicide App – www.preventsuicideapp.com/index.html
- Childline – (for people under 19) www.childline.org.uk/ tel: 0800 1111
- Silverline – (for older people) www.thesilverline.org.uk/ tel: 0800 4 70 80 90
- CALM – (for men) www.thecalmzone.net/ tel: 0800 58 58 58
- Breathing Space – (Scotland) breathingspace.scot/ tel: 0800 83 85 87
- Suicide Prevention Helpline (USA) suicidepreventionlifeline.org/ tel: 1 800 273 8255
- Crisis Services Canada – (Canada) www.crisisservicescanada.ca/ tel: 1 833 456 4566
- LifeLine – (Australia) www.lifeline.org.au/ tel: 13 11 14

Personal finances

Effective money management comes from knowing your current situation and seeking advice from experts when required so you are fully in control of your personal finances. Please consider contacting an independent financial advisor. You may find the following resources of help:

- Unbiased – UK independent financial advisor search, www. unbiased.co.uk
- NAPFA – USA independent financial advisor search, www. napfa.org
- Financial Consumer Agency of Canada – www.canada.ca/en/ financial-consumer-agency.html

- Financial Advisor Register Australia – www.moneysmart.gov.au/investing/financial-advice/financial-advisors-register
- Money Advice Service including free online budget planners – www.moneyadviceservice.org.uk/en

Relationship difficulties

If you are experiencing difficulties in your relationship, sometimes it can help for you and those involved to meet together with an independent therapist:

- Relate UK counselling support – relate.org.uk
- Better Help – Online couples counselling USA – www.betterhelp.com
- 7Cups – online relationship chat-room – www.7cups.com/relationship-advice-chat-room
- Relationships Australia – www.relationships.org.au

Bereavement support

- CRUSE Bereavement Care UK – www.cruse.org.uk
- Aftering – grief support USA – www.aftering.com/grief-support-usa
- MyGrief Canada – online bereavement support – www.mygrief.ca
- Grief Australia – support resources – www.grief.org.au/

Counselling resources

- British Association for Counselling & Psychotherapy – www.bacp.co.uk
- UK Council for Psychotherapy – www.psychotherapy.org.uk/

- UK Counselling Directory – www.counselling-directory.org.uk/
- American Counseling Association – www.counseling.org/
- Canadian Counselling & Psychotherapy Association – www.ccpa-accp.ca/
- Australian Counselling Association – www.theaca.net.au/
- International Association for Counselling – www.iac-irtac.org/

Coaching resources

- International Coach Federation – coachfederation.org/
- Association for Coaching UK – www.associationforcoaching.com/

Employee assistance providers

- Employee Assistance Professionals Association UK – www.eapa.org.uk/
- International Employee Assistance Professionals Association – www.eapassn.org/
- European Employee Assistance Forum – eaef.org/

UK National Health Service: Living well advice, tips and tools

- Eat Well – www.nhs.uk/live-well/eat-well/
- Exercise – www.nhs.uk/live-well/exercise/
- Healthy Weight – www.nhs.uk/live-well/healthy-weight/
- Sleep – www.nhs.uk/live-well/sleep-and-tiredness/
- Sexual Health – www.nhs.uk/live-well/sexual-health/

- Healthy Body – www.nhs.uk/live-well/healthy-body/
- Moodzone – www.nhs.uk/conditions/stress-anxiety-depression/
- Quit Smoking – www.nhs.uk/live-well/quit-smoking/
- Alcohol Support – www.nhs.uk/live-well/alcohol-support/

INDEX

CPSIA information can be obtained
at www.ICGtesting.com
Printed in the USA
BVHW020932250220
573261BV00012B/53